Advanced Praise for *Office Optional*

"If there was ever a time to know how to build a virtual workforce, this is it. Larry English gives you a step-by-step plan to build it out, create the right culture, and avoid costly mistakes."
—Shep Hyken, customer service and experience expert and *New York Times* bestselling author

"*Office Optional* is full of critical culture guidance and practical advice for not just running a successful virtual company but for running any company. I also run a nearly virtual company and thought I had it figured out, but Larry's book shared ideas and insights I had never considered. This is great content for the beginner as well as people already well-versed in remote working. Don't miss this timely read!"
—Lisa Stein, founder and CEO of Revolutions, Inc.

"We are wired for connection, and *Office Optional* is coming in the nick of time. Every executive, entrepreneur, and small business owner will want to read this book now. Larry serves up bite-sized strategies and tactics interlaced with engaging stories that bring to life what it's really like when you create a virtual culture, not just a virtual workforce."
—Laura Cooke, CEO of Positive Foundry

"The transition from an office to remote isn't a trend, it's our new normal. If your company can't work remotely, you can't compete. Both as an entrepreneur, and leading products within Microsoft, remote teams have been my secret weapon. They've unlocked access to top talent, speed to execution, and a cost efficiency that's helped me drive 10-times results in diverse sets of environments. In learning from Larry in *Office Optional*, I'm excited for you to make remote work your secret weapon too."

—Matthew Mottola, product leader, author of *The Human Cloud*, built the Microsoft 365 freelance toolkit

"Wherever you and your company are on the continuum of working from home, *Office Optional* is an important read. Larry shares practical lessons, specific tactics, and many detailed examples from his team in an accessible and informative approach. Centric's story emphasizes the key strategic value that results from intentionally creating and supporting a strong company culture in a virtual world. A strong culture isn't just an abstract idea in *Office Optional*. Larry brings culture creation to life with specific strategies, tactics, and stories to support the journey. When 20 years of experience is contained in such an easy-to-digest book, there is no need to invent our own unique solutions as we seek to thrive in a virtual or hybrid workplace."

—Kent Johnson, CEO of *Highlights for Children*

"It's very clear that enabling remote work is more important than ever, and that it will continue to have lasting value beyond the COVID-19 outbreak. We are committed to building the tools that help organizations, teams, and individuals stay productive and connected even when they need to work apart. Thanks to Larry and Centric for sharing how Microsoft Teams is doing just that in *Office Optional*."

—Jared Spataro, corporate vice president for Microsoft 365

"I've had the wonderful opportunity to speak to hundreds of companies. I found Centric to have not only such an enthusiastic culture of happy people, but a C-suite that was thinking ahead of the curve rather than being late adopters. Larry is so quick to create such a useful book in a time when all industries are scrambling to embrace the new frontier of remote work! He is staying ahead of the curve and ensuring collective communication and company growth through creating virtual protocol that will bond, inform, and keep everyone rocking! You go, Brother Larry!"

—Mark Schulman, drummer for P!nk, speaker, author

"*Office Optional* is a well-written and insightful look into a culturally focused virtual company. Readers of this timely book will reap the benefits of Centric's 20-year head start in defining the practices that make virtual environments rewarding for both staff members and clients. Larry English is unabashedly generous in sharing the myriad ways an organization can keep the focus on its staff as well as the company's success."

—Bill Hermann, former managing partner of Plante Moran and author of *Giving the Gift of a Career: A Roadmap for Individually Focused Staff Development*

"In *Office Optional*, Larry English shares the story of Centric Consulting's business and culture, and he lays out critical foundations for building a great culture. The Centric story is about building culture in a virtual business, but the ideas translate fully to any business. Larry and his leadership team have walked the talk of leadership and built not only a great culture, but a scalable culture. *Office Optional* is your guidebook for building a culture of trust, excellence, engagement, happiness, and fun, and this book lights the path to a high-impact culture in your business. Make no mistake, however, *Office Optional* and the ideas in it are not for the faint of heart—you must be committed, and you must be willing to get vulnerable. As Larry writes, culture is all about trust, and vulnerability is the shortcut to trust, so if you're not willing to get vulnerable, then don't bother with *Office Optional*. *Office Optional* lives culture for life."

—Jeff Nischwitz, leadership speaker, transformation coach, podcaster, and author of *Just One Step: Walking Backwards to the Present on the Camino Trail*

"*Office Optional* is a book I would recommend to all of my students as they go through the interview process. The companies and organizations in which they will build a career are increasingly likely to involve remote work. In *Office Optional*, Larry provides key insights about how people can succeed and grow in a virtual work environment. I know some of my students will become entrepreneurs. The principles of this book will serve as a wonderful template for building an environment in which their future employees will not only be productive, but feel appreciated and valued. Larry provides clear and practical guidelines and principles for building and maintaining virtual offices and remote work. More than that, he emphasizes and illustrates the vital importance of culture. This may be the most important concept that I would like for my students to learn as they are interviewing for jobs, that they should place a very high value on the culture of a company in their search. Larry and Centric Consulting clearly have created a culture in which employees can be very productive and successful while maintaining a balance in their lives that can be sustained over a career."

—Dr. James Kiper, chair of Department of Computer Science and Software Engineering at Miami University

"A thought-provoking read for any business leader who has been thrust into creating a virtual work environment without losing the office culture. *Office Optional* skillfully articulates how to practically apply strategies to allow the company culture to thrive without being in an office together. Larry English and the Centric team provide stories throughout the book to show the confidence business leaders need to begin embracing new ways of working, office optional."

—David O'Toole, director of program strategy at World Wide Technology, Inc.

"In today's global work environment, organizations and their employees must effectively communicate across different locations, time zones, and languages to drive their businesses forward. Microsoft Teams puts everything organizations need—chats, meetings, calling, and Office 365 apps—to make faster, more informed decisions in a single, intelligent hub. Thanks to Larry for sharing how Teams is doing this across Centric in *Office Optional*."

—Lori Wright, general manager of Microsoft 365

"As a strategic gifting expert, I'm always looking for content from like-minded people, and Larry English is one of them. His book, *Office Optional*, will help any leader learn how to create impactful experiences for clients and employees, even when you don't see each other every day, or even every month."

—John Ruhlin, CEO and author of *Giftology*

"Larry has done a terrific job in sharing ideas and concepts that can help anyone leading or operating in a remote workforce environment. Like any great recipe, you can adjust the ingredients to your corporate taste and end up with a very satisfying dish. Over the past four years, I've had the pleasure of seeing firsthand the Centric team deliver results both domestically and internationally. They truly live their differentiating culture at scale, regardless if an associate is based in Gurgaon, India, or Columbus, Ohio. Kudos to Larry and his team for being ahead of the curve in navigating the remote workforce landscape."

—Timothy J. Cunningham, VP and chief information officer for Grange Insurance

"*Official Optional* outlines and discusses critical components of building a successful remote and virtual operation. Building culture and trust in a remote environment are keys to success, and Larry illustrates how to focus and implement these strategies beautifully. As the CEO of a fully remote company myself, I highly recommend this book whether you are new to remote work or you already run a remote company. There are amazing takeaways found in *Office Optional!*"

—Liza Rodewald, CEO and founder of Instant Teams

Office Optional

Hardcover ISBN: 9781735056715
Paperback ISBN: 9781735056722
Ebook ISBN: 9781735056708

Book design by Carolina VonKampen
Author photo by Jennifer Korman
Graphic in chapter 9 designed by Centric

Office Optional

How to Build a Connected Culture with Virtual Teams

Larry English

Published by Centric Consulting

To Centric employees past and present who have all contributed to our unmatched culture

CONTENTS

INTRODUCTION

Crap, We've Started a Virtual Company

I was excited. We had our first client, and I was presenting the final deliverable on a conference call to stakeholders who were spread out around the country. I was at home in my office, on speakerphone to keep my hands free. The presentation was going well.

My office had the kind of French doors where the handles don't turn—you simply push to open them. My young son, still in potty-training mode, burst through the doors and came running into my office. I had no time to react before he loudly proclaimed, "Daddy, I've gotta poop, and you are going to wipe me!" Just like the movies, it felt like slow motion as I lunged for the mute button—but I was much too late.

—Larry E., Columbus, Ohio

We Accidentally Found the Future of Work

I had a midlife crisis at 25.

All of the Centric founders, myself included, went to work for one of the big international consulting companies out of college. I learned a lot quickly, but I also worked 80 to 100 hours a week, including weekends.

After five years of this pace, I had one of those life-changing, lightbulb moments. I was leaving work at 10 p.m., walking out of a dark office to a deserted parking lot. I thought, "Is this all there is to life? I'm going to work nonstop, retire, and die?" I needed a break to try to figure out how I was going to live my life. So, I took a leave of absence. My newlywed wife and I bought a one-way ticket to Iceland and spent the next year wandering around the world.

We were about eight months into the trip, lying on a beach in Bali, when I read a quote that would change my life. In *The Drifters*, James Michener wrote, "Southern Florida is filled with people sixty-eight years old who were going to do something big in their lives but waited until it was safe. Now it's safe and they're sixty-eight years old." I immediately knew I had to take a risk and try to do something big.

I returned home and joined a startup that was sold to a dot-com publicly traded company. Both companies were all about the money, trying to get to an exit as soon as possible and hitting aggressive earnings goals. Things like culture were an afterthought. I still hadn't found the answer.

I reconnected with my like-minded coworkers from my early days of working all those late hours. We were lamenting why all the businesses we had encountered were focused on profit first and people second. They had boring and sterile cultures. They had politics and games. Were we destined to be miserable the rest of our careers?

It finally hit us. Why can't we create a place that we love to work? Why can't we create a business that doesn't kill people for profit? We began dreaming up a company where we could do great work but still have a life, a company with a fun culture that treats everyone like family and operates with honest and deep relationships. This was the start of the Centric business model and the underpinnings of the culture we have today.

As we were developing our initial business model, we felt going virtual could provide better balance in the lives of our consultants and be more cost-effective. Equally important, we decided that a strong, fun culture was possible even if employees were untethered to a traditional office.

That was 20 years ago. Since then, we've grown to nearly 1,000 employees with operations in 12 US cities and India, all working remotely some or most of the time. Being virtual has become second nature, and we've proven that it works for the business and it works for our employees, who can live a better, balanced lifestyle with more flexibility. (As an added bonus, we've saved millions in rent over the years.)

> "In thirty years' time, as technology moves forward even further, people are going to look back and wonder why offices ever existed."
> —Richard Branson | Founder, Virgin Group

At Centric, how people interact with coworkers and clients has become more complex over time. Some employees work on-site at clients' offices, and some work with remote client teams. We spin up office space when it's needed for a client requirement or to train new hires just out of college. We have employees in India who work remotely to avoid the tough commute in Delhi, and our entire back office staff and most of our leadership team work completely virtually. When the coronavirus pandemic hit, for example, we were completely virtual within one day. Our work can get done and done well with any combination of these scenarios.

We used to call remote work the model of the future. The reality is, it's already here. Historically, companies have been slow to embrace remote work, but the coronavirus pandemic in 2020 accelerated its adoption. When the outbreak hit (right when we were in the process of publishing this book), many companies were forced to go remote overnight. They quickly recognized the value in remote work in maintaining continuity when things like natural disasters or global pandemics occur.

Moving forward, learning to work remotely and maintaining a connected culture is not only going to be critical to success—it will be the new normal. The good news is technology has made remote collaboration easy, and workers appreciate the work-life benefits it brings, too.

Even before the coronavirus outbreak, all signs pointed to remote work rapidly gaining traction:

- 69 percent of Gen Z and millennial managers let their team members work remotely[1]

- 23 percent of workers reported doing some portion of their work remotely[2]

- It's predicted that by 2028, 73 percent of all departments will have remote workers[3]

Operating virtually certainly has its challenges, like young kids bursting into your office. But we believe that most companies will have to embrace virtual work to attract and keep the best talent: 71 percent of workers say the option to work remotely would be a deciding factor in choosing a job, and 75 percent say being able to work remotely would encourage them to stick around longer.[4]

Plus, I suspect many workers who got a taste of remote work during the coronavirus pandemic are going to want the option of working from home at least some of the time moving forward. And the secret to remote work success comes down to one thing: culture.

We Stumbled into Why Culture Matters

"Culture eats strategy for breakfast."
—Peter Drucker | Father of management theory

Over the years, countless books have been written on the value of culture. We did not read any of them before starting our company. All of us experienced an incredible amount of stress in our previous roles, and while starting a new business can certainly create its own kind of stress, we didn't want to bring those old pain points into our new company. And we certainly didn't want our future employees to experience the same.

We just wanted to create a great environment. A couple of years in, we looked around and realized how happy we were. We loved everyone we worked with. Turns out work is actually fun when you can feed off the energy of a positive environment.

Over time, we've realized that having a great culture does more than make work enjoyable. It's actually a big competitive advantage. A Gallup study estimates that companies with a highly engaged culture see a 59 percent higher revenue per employee than the average company.[5] Happy employees provide amazing customer service, stay with the company longer, and attract great new hires.

Once we realized how critical culture was to our success, we refined our vision to create an unmatched culture in the industry. We began to actively invest in culture and manage it. Over time, our culture started to win awards, such as Glassdoor's Employee's Choice Award for Best Places to Work and many best places to work awards. We believe this is our secret sauce that has helped us generate great growth: We have been listed on the Inc. 5000 seven times.

So what is culture? It's the personality of a company. It defines the environment in which employees work and includes both the spoken and unspoken rules for how things get done in a company. This book focuses on culture and how you build that culture when you have some portion of your workforce working virtually.

Why Read This Book?

This book is designed to be your remote culture guide, showing you how to build a great culture when you have to virtually interact with employees in many different ways to get work done.

When we tell the story about our culture and explain that we operate virtually, we often get confused looks. We wrote this book to explain how we did it so others can take away ideas on building a strong culture when they operate virtually. We hope to add our story to what we believe will be a major area of study in the future.

This book is written for any business leader who is managing partial or totally remote teams and wants to understand what they need to do to build a strong culture. This book is also for anyone who wants to become a successful remote team member.

Throughout these pages, you'll learn about building culture for all types of remote work situations (e.g., all team members are virtual, a hybrid model with some workers in an office and some working remotely, teams spread out over the globe).

How the Rest of the Book Is Structured

We've tried to make this book fun, quick to read, and readily actionable.

We've included many embarrassing stories of our struggles to find the right formula. We hope our candor is not only entertaining, but also helps you avoid some of our mistakes and illustrates that building culture is not easy, but nevertheless can be a fun (although never-finished) journey.

The chapters are presented in the order of how you would think through building culture when you are either starting to put together a virtual team from scratch or when you have suddenly inherited a virtual team. Each chapter ends with summaries, quick lists of actions you can take immediately, and challenges you will face.

- Chapter 1 covers trust, the foundation of any successful virtual company

- Chapter 2 walks you through how to discover, define, and refine your virtual culture

- Chapter 3 communicates the importance of hiring employees who are natural fits for your culture

- Chapter 4 tells you how to go about recruiting for culture

- Chapter 5 is about training your employees on your culture

- Chapter 6 defines how to build strong virtual relationships

- Chapter 7 illustrates how to design impactful in-person interactions

- Chapter 8 shows you how to use feedback to improve your culture

- Chapter 9 describes tools you will need to create a virtual culture

- Chapter 10 explains how to be a great virtual team member

1

Remote Work 101: It's All about Trust

The company was up and running with remote workers, and it was going well. And then we ran into the issue that is the biggest initial worry of anyone who is starting to manage remote workers: An employee "went dark."

Countless emails, phone calls, and voicemails—no response. No information was available from family or friends. As days passed, our concerns heightened. Should we file a missing person report? Check the hospitals?

When we exhausted all other ideas, I decided to go to the employee's house, hoping it would not be uncomfortable for the employee, or worse, that I would find something had happened to her. I knocked on the front door but got no answer. Did I have the right house? Maybe she just stepped out for food? Should I wait in my car until she returned?

As I settled back into my car with nothing to do, it hit me—this was my first official stakeout! I'd seen them on TV but underestimated the complexity. Based on the awkward glances from passersby, I was clearly lacking the skills to look inconspicuous. Pretend phone calls and searching for imaginary objects in my car clearly wasn't cutting it.

Minutes turned to hours. So I did what any good consultant would do and established my own stakeout best practices—things like periodically moving the car, getting out and checking the tires, opening the hood, checking the oil, making more fake phone calls—basically looking like a cat burglar casing the entire neighborhood.

The good news was nobody called the cops, our employee eventually returned home and was okay, and my stakeout skills have since atrophied. But we did learn that not everyone is able to work in a virtual company!

—Jeff L., Cincinnati, Ohio

Don't Try This at Home

When business leaders consider a remote workforce, their immediate worry is that virtual employees will simply not work as hard as they would under in-person supervision. The reality is that situations like the story above are *incredibly* rare. We have worked with thousands of people over the last 20 years and can count on our hands how many times we've had an issue where someone was intentionally not working.

Most everyone can work from home. Many people actually find that their productivity increases, and nearly a third say they are able to work more efficiently without the distractions of an office.[1]

Research aside, lack of trust in remote workers remains a common mistake companies make when they start building a remote work force. They waste money on tools that monitor when the employee is sitting at their desk, what apps they are using, and what sites they are visiting. If you want to build a great culture and are going to take this approach, there is no need to read the rest of this book. No one is happy when they are not trusted. You will have a culture, but it won't be good and certainly not great.

Many companies also mistakenly assume their management and measurement structures need to be revamped for virtual workers. This is simply not true, but you may want to baseline productivity before launching a virtual team and compare the results afterward.

Based on my experience, you can completely trust your team when you aren't directly observing them. Research backs this up: Organizations with high-trust cultures have been found to have 50 percent lower turnover rates; greater stock market returns; and increased innovation, engagement, and organizational agility.[2] Employees with high-trust organizations also feel 74 percent less stressed, 50 percent more productive, 106 percent more energetic, and 29 percent more satisfied with their lives.[3]

In the rare case that someone isn't getting their work done, we've been able to tell quickly. Just like a brick-and-mortar company, if you have a good management structure in place and are reviewing work product at an appropriate pace, when someone isn't performing, it shows up immediately.

The biggest issue we face is usually the exact opposite: Employees end up working *too* much because they do not have the natural break of going into and leaving the office (more on this in chapter 10). Also, if someone hasn't worked remotely before, there's usually an adjustment period as they figure out how to make it work for their home environment and schedule. Those who are initially reluctant to make the switch usually love it once they get their new routine down.

When we do encounter a problem, it is an extreme rarity that it has anything to do with the person working virtually. Instead, the issues tend to be normal employee development snags that should be addressed the same as if they were working in an office. If we need to deliver a hard message, we schedule a face-to-face meeting or a video call.

To start building your remote culture, establish and share some basic rules. The first and most important rule is mutual trust between the company and its workers. The rules after that? As few as possible. Tell your employees they will be treated like adults with the flexibility to get the job done however is best for them. Of course, different types of businesses have constraints on when an employee needs to be available. Depending on the job type, we try to give employees the ability to work whatever hours are best for them.

DO Try This at Home

I joined Centric in late August 2017. When I rejoined my previous organization after maternity leave, my kid was only four months old. Due to issues related to maternity, feeding, care, and the long commute in Delhi, I was unable to give proper time to my child and decided to put my career on hold. While I enjoyed my time as a full-time mother with my infant, I also found I missed my individuality and professional life. After a while, I started searching for a new job either near my home or near a nursery facility.

Fortunately, I found Centric. Working from home has been a boon for me. I have the freedom to work at any time and from anywhere and, therefore, it's become manageable for me to take care of my child while having a professional life, too.

—Ruchika G., Gurgaon, India

This story illustrates the power of a virtual workforce: a talented woman in India is able to continue her career, collaborate with team members around the world, avoid a time-wasting commute, and have the proper work-life balance to raise her child.

But it's not just the worker who benefits. The company benefits greatly, as well. In fact, according to a Stanford study, telecommuters take fewer breaks, sick days, and time off, and they have half the attrition rate of in-office workers.[4] A 2016 study also found that 91 percent of remote workers feel they're more productive.[5]

In other words, this research proves what we've always found true at Centric: you can work remotely with people anywhere in the world, get work done with greater productivity, *and* have a strong culture.

Translating Trust into Great Culture

Trust in your employees is essential for remote work success. It also forms the underlying foundation of a great virtual culture. Here are two stories that help explain.

One of the stories I rely upon when talking about the Centric culture is how work-life balance is a real thing and the flexibility we employees have. I had the opportunity to coach my daughter's high school soccer team, which meant leaving work around 2:30 every afternoon during the fall season. This was possible because of the relationship my team had with my client along with the trust Centric had in me. I was able to have a great experience with my daughter's team and still fulfill my client expectations in a nontraditional manner. This flexibility continues today as I occasionally spend time during the work week teaching adaptive sports to the disabled population. I am grateful to my company for having and maintaining great cultural standards and out-of-the-box thinking that is empowered by trust and flexibility.

—Gwenn D., Columbus, Ohio

***

One of the primary reasons I chose to work at Centric, aside from the incredible people, was the company's "self-managed" paid time off (PTO) policy. When I first heard about this, I was amazed; never had an employer showed so much trust in my ability to manage my own time. With great joy, I balanced my time off by working extra hours with no intervention on the part of management to ask me where I had been last Tuesday at 10 o'clock.

Three years in to my employment at Centric, a friend from college began to fill my head with delusions of grandeur about hiking the Appalachian Trail, a 2,200-mile trail stretching from Georgia to Maine. I became infatuated with the idea. I recalled from my employee handbook that part of Centric's self-managed PTO policy was the ability to take a three-month leave of absence. This policy was so unbelievable to me that I had to meet with the president to confirm the company's support.

I made arrangements with my client and everyone I worked with. When I presented the idea to leadership, they had the utmost trust in the arrangements I had made, never questioning if I "needed" the time or if the plans I had made with the client were acceptable. To the contrary, every leader I spoke to seemed to share my excitement at the prospect of fulfilling a dream. The only questions I received were in regard to my survival on such a treacherous vacation.

I did survive, hiking 900 miles of Appalachian Trail with my friend over the course of my leave of absence. It was a life-changing experience. To this day, I'm filled with happiness and gratitude to have walked those miles and to have been welcomed back by both my leaders and my client.

—Kyle B., Columbus, Ohio

As you can see, by starting with trust and allowing remote employees great autonomy and flexibility to manage their time, people get to be independent and empowered while still feeling like a part of something bigger. In the two stories above, you can sense how delighted employees are to have flexibility. This leads to happy, loyal employees with a rich quality of life, which leads to an amazing culture.

Building Trust between Team Members

While trusting your employees is important, employees also need to trust each other. Many of us have been in organizations where this doesn't occur, and politics win the day instead of the best idea. Coworkers talk behind each other's backs, and you don't know who you can trust. This leads to a toxic culture, unhappy employees, and bad results.

It's on the company to prevent this by facilitating trust between coworkers. Trust is particularly critical when building culture in a remote environment because virtual workers are unable to read all the visual cues that you get face-to-face. If they trust one another, they'll give their colleagues the benefit of the doubt and have more patience to work through tough problems and any communication issues that arise.

At Centric, we've fostered trust between coworkers in a virtual environment by:

- Incorporating natural ways for employees to build deeper relationships that foster trust. This is covered in chapters 6 and 7 on building virtual relationships and maximizing face-to-face interactions when they occur.

- Teaching everyone to assume good intent. If something doesn't feel right, ask respectful questions to understand the other person's perspective. Always start with the assumption that your coworker is trying to do the right thing.

- Asking people to talk to each other one-on-one if they are having an issue, rather than going over their head to a supervisor or complaining to a coworker. Yes, this is super hard to teach. People naturally want to avoid conflict. To help, we offer employees curriculum based on the book *Crucial Conversations*.[6] This provides a roadmap for having conversations when the stakes or emotions are high.

- Having a zero-tolerance policy for politics. If we see it, we call it out and coach that person on how to create a positive environment.

Trust is some powerful magic. When you know your coworkers have your back, you are at ease to focus on doing your best work. Everyone doing their best work leads to dynamic teams that accomplish amazing things. Being part of a high-performing team that you are excited to engage with creates a strong culture people want to be a part of. In other words, trust fuels a cycle of happy, productive employees, great work, and an amazing culture.

Quick Read Summary

- The underlying foundation of a great virtual culture is trust in all your remote workers. Don't worry that remote employees will not work hard. This is an extremely rare situation, and, in fact, remote workers tend to work harder than their in-office counterparts!

- When you begin allowing employees to work remotely, simply allow them to work from home. Don't overcomplicate it. In the rare case that someone isn't getting their work done, we've been able to tell quickly. Just like a brick-and-mortar company, if you have a good management structure in place and are reviewing work product at an appropriate pace, when someone isn't performing, it shows up immediately.

- Starting with trust and giving employees great autonomy and flexibility allows people to feel independent and empowered while still feeling like a part of something bigger.

This leads to happy, loyal employees with a rich quality of life, which in turn leads to an amazing culture.

How to Get Started Building a Culture of Trust

- Establish as few rules for working remotely as possible—the idea is to treat people like responsible adults who can govern their own time.

- Encourage employees to trust one another, to assume good intent, and to pick up the phone if they sense an issue is brewing.

Challenges You Will Encounter

- You will have people reluctant to work from a home office. We've had many objections, but once someone starts doing it, they never want to go back.

- Employees who work remotely tend to work too much. We discuss how to address this in chapter 10, which covers being a great virtual employee.

- You must have strong leaders to help encourage people to resolve issues themselves. This is difficult to achieve—we address this more fully in chapter 6.

2

Digging Deep to Discover Your Virtual Culture

Shortly after starting with Centric Consulting, I decided to rejoin the military after a 10-year break in service. The vice president of my team was behind me 100 percent, but as a company, Centric had not been down this path before. I worked with human resources and legal to create guidelines to address individuals who want to serve their country. Together we created a policy that is fair to everyone involved.

In 2010, I was sent on a nine-month deployment to support Operation New Dawn in Iraq. Centric supported me in numerous ways during this time. They continued to pay my salary at a differential rate and sent numerous care packages, messages, and emails, ensuring that I and my fellow Security Forces airmen were taken care of. They even looked after my family by offering to cut my lawn and help my wife with childcare. Lastly, upon my return, they presented my family with a paid weekend away so we could spend some much-needed quality time together.

We talk about force multipliers in the military, and I never thought of my employer as a force multiplier, but in this case they definitely were. I am so grateful for what they have done for me, my family, and the country.

—Mike R., Columbus, Ohio

***

A couple of years ago, I was working on-site with a client in a loud and often difficult work environment. We were having one of those tough days where you learn 10 new requirements and your way forward seems blocked. It snowed most of the day, so I decided to leave a little early to clear my car so I could make it to my late afternoon client meeting.

Suddenly, it hit me. We'd all had a bad day—why should anyone else have to deal with scraping their cars? I smiled and turned this chore into a happy experience by clearing the cars around me.

I'd cleared about four cars when someone else came out of the building and waved and smiled as they passed me. I went over and knocked on their window, saying I wanted to clear their car because I was already knee-deep into the experience. I will never forget the gratitude they shared with me. It was magical!

I could have cleared cars the rest of the afternoon, but I had a meeting to get to. Off I went, dripping wet but smiling all the way, hoping that my coworkers would have one less thing to contend with at the end of their day!

—Karen A., St. Louis, Missouri

Trust is a given when trying to build a great virtual culture, but there are other essential components to consider. At its core, a virtual culture is no different than that of traditional in-office companies: It's the set of spoken and unspoken rules for how things get done. The only difference is you need to layer in some extra considerations to ensure your culture extends to employees who log on from home.

Even if you feel you already have a well-defined culture, you will still find this section provides valuable pointers on improving or refining it.

Centric's "Why"

Often, companies don't take the time to figure out what their culture is. We were no different. We founded Centric on a few basic core ideas and principles; all we knew was that everyone loved working at the company.

Later on, we began attempting to define our culture and what made working at Centric special. It was a struggle. We began with documenting our core purpose, the "why" behind our existence. After nine months, we had just two measly, uninspiring, forgettable paragraphs.

Needing help, we turned to an approach by Jim Collins and Jerry Porras called "Building Your Company's Vision." [1] One of their techniques to help you suss out your purpose has you answer five "why" questions. First you define your product or service. Then you ask, "Why is that important?" Repeat the question five times, drilling down deeper with each iteration.

By the end of this exercise, we finally got it right: Our "why" is to create unmatched customer and employee experiences. Turns out, we were living our core purpose, our culture, all along. We just didn't know how to articulate it—it never seemed like a big deal.

The stories at the beginning of this chapter illustrate what we mean by "unmatched experiences"—we make it a point to thoughtfully go beyond what is expected to create an incomparable experience for each other and our clients. We don't do this because we want anything in return. We do it because we find it personally rewarding, a great way to live, and our chosen path to an amazing culture. Performing small, thoughtful gestures deepens relationships we have with each other. Our "why" is our North Star, our secret sauce, and a big part of what makes Centric unique.

Discovering Your Culture

Defining and embracing your "why" is just the first step of discovering your culture. The building blocks detailed below will help you further refine it. We'll give an overview of each and provide an example from our own culture. Taking the time to think through these components and write down how your company approaches each one will grant you clarity in your culture. The exercise will help you maintain your culture as your business evolves and ensure you extend it to your virtual workers (more on that later on).

Core values

> Centric gives out an advance to our profit-sharing bonus in late November. I had just been hired to start the St. Louis team, so I was totally shocked to be included. I was too new to have had any major impact, and I felt I did not deserve it. But to the company leaders, I was part of our shared success. It was just the fair way they did things.

This generosity and commitment to treating everyone as part of the team inspired me to donate the entire bonus to a local food bank in Centric's name.

This experience also helped me live our core value of committing to impact our communities and the greater good. For the last six years, I have been honored to keep up and expand this tradition, donating my November bonus to organizations that are important to members of our team. It has become my favorite tradition and a large part of my love for Centric.

—Paul H., St. Louis, Missouri

The values you authentically live as a company form the foundation of your culture. They underlie everything you do, from making decisions and policies to hiring and rewarding employees. Ideally, your core values should include a handful of timeless principles. We have seven, one of which is igniting passion for the greater good and committing to improve the world we live in, as the story above illustrates.

Since we wrote down our core values 15 years ago, they have not changed. Many people we hire are surprised that the values we publicly acknowledge are the values we actually live day to day. This is surprisingly rare in the business world. For example, recall how Enron's stated values (communication, integrity, respect, excellence) couldn't have been further from how they actually operated.[2] It all starts at the top—as a leader, your job is to authentically live and model your values for your employees.

Traditions

> We have a tradition during our spring meeting. Just when attention is waning, up pops an embarrassing photo of one of the company leaders from when they were younger. The first time I saw this, I thought "Wow, the way they choose to humble themselves and lighten up the environment is so cool!"
>
> One year later, the conversation at the meeting shifted to great things going on in Chicago, my team. And THERE IT WAS ON THE SCREEN! Me, at my sister's wedding, well beyond my limit of alcohol consumption, no shirt, pink tuxedo suspenders, long hair, handlebar mustache, doing my very best Chippendales-meets-Tom Selleck imitation. So many thoughts ran through my head . . . wow . . . I looked pretty buff then . . . bad choice of outfit. . . . But the roars of my Centric associates interrupted my thoughts. Everyone was laughing, but not at me. We were laughing together.
>
> —Jim M., Chicago, Illinois

The traditions your company holds dear speak volumes about what you value in your culture. Traditions can include how your company celebrates a big sales win, when someone is hired or promoted, when someone retires, and events like holidays, birthdays, and births.

We have many traditions big and small. My personal favorite is our annual holiday party. For no other reason than to have fun and celebrate the year, we fly all employees and their significant others or guest for a long weekend of fun in the winter. Other traditions include sending Mother's Day and Father's Day gifts, inviting employees to audition for the Centric band that plays at our spring meeting, and me personally calling every person who gets promoted. All of these traditions enhance and reinforce our culture.

The look and feel

All of the things you can physically see about a company are also part of its culture. This includes the way employees dress, the look and feel of your office space (if you have it), your internal and external websites, the awards you share, and your logos and branding.

At Centric, we have a laid-back, comfortable culture, and many things reflect that. A big one is dress code, such as this employee discovered:

> The first consulting firm I joined maintained a
> dress code that not only included tailored business suits, French cuffed Oxford shirts, neckties,

and dress shoes, but also stipulated what colors and styles were appropriate for each item. If we were visiting a manufacturing plant or rail yards and it was recommended we dress casual, this meant losing the suit and tie for khakis and a blazer.

When I first joined Centric, I knew the culture was casual, but it wasn't until my first spring meeting that I truly understood what this meant. Seeing the entire organization in T-shirts and jeans was shocking to me. I stuck out as "the new guy" in a blazer. Many people, including Larry, encouraged me to lose the jacket.

At the summer meeting, I allowed myself to wear jeans, but I didn't feel comfortable enough to wear a T-shirt. Larry spotted me in my button-down and dress shoes and threw down the gauntlet. "At the next spring meeting, I want you to wear a hoodie," he said.

When the next spring meeting rolled around, I had learned enough about Centric to know that everyone is willing to have a good laugh at themselves. I walked up to Larry wearing a hoodie underneath a navy blazer. I informed Larry that I didn't feel any more casual, and he remembered the challenge and started laughing and introduced me to those around him.

—David B., St. Louis, Missouri

Unwritten rules

I had boarded a plane bound for our spring meeting in St. Louis. As the last travelers took their seats, I received a call from my wife and heard the words that no one wants to hear: "The doctors think it is cancer." My colleagues immediately started providing the "unmatched experience" that we have all come to enjoy at Centric.

I knew I needed to return home as soon as possible, but I was unable to exit the plane. My colleague and good friend called his wife, and she immediately identified return flight options. Upon landing in St. Louis, I knew exactly where to go and what flight to book home.

Support for my wife and me has continued from that day forward. Throughout chemotherapy, surgery, and radiation, Centric has supported us through cards and visits. They also organized an event to prepare a number of meals that I could easily make with minimal effort. (My wife and daughters certainly appreciated that.)

Given the reassurance that family comes first, I was able to provide the care that my wife and family needed during this difficult time while still balancing my work responsibilities. My

partners took on my workload even though
they were already working more than 40 hours
per week. I can never express the gratitude to
my colleagues who are now truly part of my extended family.

—Brad S., Columbus, Ohio

Every company has many unwritten rules, the
things everyone knows and does but aren't detailed in
an HR manual. Taking the time to think through these
unwritten rules will help you discover this facet of your
culture.

For example, we try to hire employees for life. We
recognize that everyone will have times in their personal life when they need support, so one of our unwritten rules, as the story above illustrates, is that we do
whatever it takes to support an employee through a life
hurdle, whether that means letting them work reduced
hours or everyone chipping in to get their work done.
This rule is not written down anywhere, but all of our
leadership and HR staff know to live it. When these
kinds of events occur, we rise to the occasion without
missing a beat.

Who succeeds

The behaviors and attributes of who succeeds and who
doesn't in your organization are also important facets
of your culture. Our superstars tend to be individuals

who are great collaborators and humble, trustworthy leaders, people who live our values and are great at building relationships.

To define who succeeds at your company, ask yourself the following questions:

- **Who gets hired?** What attributes and criteria are you looking for when you're hiring someone new?

- **Who gets promoted?** What types of behaviors does your company reward? What are the key promotion criteria? What are the attributes of your leadership?

- **Who doesn't work out?** What skills or personality traits are they missing? What behavior is a contributor?

Operating philosophies

Operating philosophies are just what they sound like: principles your company lives by in how it operates. To have a strong culture, your operating philosophy should align with your core values.

One of our operating philosophies is to remain private. We intentionally set up the company to be private, versus publicly traded or sold, because we believe we can better live our values and execute our long-term plan by not having to focus on quarterly financial goals and nonstop growth expectations. We also believe in idea meritocracy—we always want the best idea to win and not always cede to the highest-ranked or most vocal person in the meeting. In pursuit of this, we de-emphasize the importance of titles and model nonemotional debate and balanced discussion of our ideas to make sure we always land at the best answer.

Virtual Components of Culture

Once you've rolled up your sleeves and done the hard work of thinking through and defining your core culture, you can begin layering in the necessary virtual elements. Whether you have just a few virtual team members or are starting a totally virtual company, you'll need to think through how remote workers are integrated into your culture and ways being virtual can actually enhance your culture.

This is an important step, as virtual work requires different processes and changes the way employees interact with one another. To help you work through the many considerations of taking your culture virtual, I'll lay out Centric's approach below.

Embrace the realities of working from home

On Fridays, I often get back from my morning workout just in time for our early morning leadership call. If I have an in-person meeting afterward, I don't have enough time to shower and make it to the meeting. So, I sometimes shower while on the conference call, placing my phone on speaker and mute and setting it on a high ledge in the shower where it won't get wet. The hard part comes when I'm asked a question and have to turn off the shower and respond covered in soap.

At one of our company get-togethers, we were having a few drinks and talking about crazy places we have taken calls. I shared my morning shower story. Big mistake! I will never live this down. But I have to admit that the jokes and ribbing are well deserved and, on the bright side, very creative.

—Centric employee who obviously prefers to remain anonymous

Barking dogs, interrupting kids, ringing doorbells, a kid's soccer game in the background—when you have a virtual workforce, you have to make it okay for people to encounter these and other hazards of not being in an office building. (But showering on a call may be pushing it.)

Of course, for an important client call, you will have to find a place that will be quiet with no interruptions. But it is important to recognize that employees are working remotely and these background noises and interruptions are expected. No one should be embarrassed or called out for it. We also set the same expectations with our clients.

At Centric, we actually call out these quirks of working remote and make it part of the dialogue. I've taken many calls at my son's golf matches and had to talk in a "golf voice." I'll intersperse my best Jim Nantz play-by-play commentary if the call needs energy. We've had people take calls from every conceivable location, from horse shows and hockey games to grade school holiday parties and the carpool lane. And it's all okay.

Promote life flexibility

> Alarm. Loud. 5:20 a.m. Really? The river? Really. Half cup coffee in mug, two cups coffee in thermos. Grab dog. Drive three miles to the Griggs Reservoir dock.
>
> Arrive. 5:45 a.m. Mate's there on time, as usual. Boat positioned on ramp. Back boat into water. Load dog. Fire up the trusty 1999 Ski Nautique 196. Drive boat 20 minutes to the course.
>
> This symphony of water-skiing precision has repeated itself hundreds of times over the last 10 years. Executed only by the truly dedicated: the course skiers. Those who like to ski the slalom course, 34 miles per hour, wake crossing at over 50 miles per hour, through the entry gate, around six turn balls, through exit gates. Make it? Then shorten the rope and try again. Who will best the competition this morning?

Why so early? Because the course is on a river only five miles from downtown Columbus. Public water that gets busy as the day grows longer. You have to get out there early. When it's perfect. And quiet. Sun coming up. Mist on the water. The day breaking.

6:15 a.m. First skier in the water. That would be me. Because I was the last one to get on board with Water Ski Wednesday 10 years ago. So, I go first, every time. Cold, often shockingly so. Water colder than air? Air colder than water?

6:35 a.m. Done. Six to eight passes through the course. 16.95 seconds gate to gate with six turns in between. Thrilling, dangerous, physical, beautiful. Yes, the river. Every Wednesday. Yes, yes, yes. 5:20 a.m.? Can do.

7:30 a.m. Back at dock. Everyone's had their turn. And no matter how well you skied, it's always excellent. The beauty of the river, God's creation on display. What a way to start the workday. In the office by 8:30 a.m., already dreaming of the next early alarm on ski day.

—Mike B., Columbus, Ohio

We want everyone to have the flexibility to manage when they get work done and when they do the things outside of work that are important to them—whether it's water-skiing every Wednesday morning or coaching their kid's basketball team. We make sure to communicate this flexibility to employees. We let them know it is not only accepted but expected that their day might not hew to the traditional eight-to-five. We don't want employees to feel guilty or feel like they need to hide that they are doing a nonwork activity in the middle of the day.

When you promote this kind of flexible virtual environment, you have to set different expectations for how work is done. Work may not be delivered in the normal window. Calls or emails may not be returned right away. The expectations may vary by job type, but the important idea is to embrace the benefits that being virtual creates for employees. Build those benefits into your expectations about how work is delivered. Let employees know that they don't have to call you back immediately, that they absolutely should go to their kid's school to read to the class or take that midday yoga class.

Build opportunities for human connection

> When we started Centric St. Louis, I was lucky enough to be reunited with one of my favorite former colleagues, Paul. We partnered in developing our pipeline, growing our team, delivering top-notch work to our clients, and establishing an exceptional, warm, family-like, sustainable culture.

This was an awesome opportunity, and ridiculously fun. It was also stressful and a ton of work. Paul and I needed to find balance. As partners, we needed to spend time together strategizing our future and building our vision. As friends, we needed to get together to empathize with one another, support each other, and blow off some steam.

Early on, we made it a priority to regularly connect in person, usually in the form of a weekly happy hour over margaritas at a local Mexican restaurant. We would share our highs and lows, talk about our families, discuss our real-life challenges and fears, and occasionally allow ourselves to celebrate our early success. This was the highlight of our week.

As time went on, Paul and I became busier . . . and busier . . . and busier. We were both running in different directions and had less time to get together in person. We couldn't always prioritize our time together over other needs, but we knew we needed to somehow maintain that connection. Enter the virtual happy hour.

Virtual happy hour sounds counterintuitive, right? How can a happy hour be virtual? But here's the thing about happy hours. The drinks are fun, and the one-on-one time is important. But more than margaritas, the beauty of my happy hour with Paul was—and is—finding time to connect as colleagues, friends, and humans. To go beyond business, beyond the transactional, and spend time on the things that really matter.

Where we are sitting or whether we have a drink in hand is inconsequential. A scheduled call or video chat on a Friday afternoon allows Paul and I to take a few minutes to deliberately and purposefully connect, to mix in the fun stories from our week as well as the challenges we've faced. It gives us time to celebrate and be vulnerable, to find the balance between work and play, family and work. It reinforces our friendship and our partnerships. For that, we say, "Cheers!"

—Jen B., St. Louis, Missouri

Virtual meetings are where all of the work gets done in a virtual company. It's where relationships are built and your culture is reinforced, so it's important to develop a structure and protocol for virtual meetings. Considerations need to include how meetings will be structured, what format they'll take, when they'll need to be in person and when virtual is okay, and how you'll handle sensitive topics.

Our rules for virtual meetings include:

Make room for personal connection. On virtual calls, allow time for relationship building and vulnerability. As a leader, it's your job to model this. Our meetings always begin with a kind of virtual watercooler sharing. Sometimes we include an agenda item where everyone shares their highest high and lowest low for the month. Some moderators kick off meetings with a question like "What is the grossest food you have ever eaten?" or "If you could have any superpower, what would it be and why?" Either way, for the first five minutes or so, we talk on a personal level before diving into business.

Require engagement. We have all been guilty of being distracted on a call. Suddenly you hear your name and have to beg for forgiveness and ask them to bring you up to speed. So while we want people to have flexibility, we also believe if you are going to be on a call, you owe it to everyone to be just as engaged as if you were all in the same room. If you are doing something that will cause you to be distracted, we just ask that you let everyone know at the beginning of the call. This is one of those unwritten rules we all naturally follow—engagement and consideration for others are baked into our culture.

Encourage, but don't require, video. Some companies require video for every call. Centric doesn't. As part of our commitment to flexibility, we recognize that people might be in a car or haven't showered yet that day, so we have always made video optional. That said, seeing someone's facial expressions has definite advantages. You have to decide what will work best for your company.

Handle emotionally charged topics carefully. It's a fact of business that sometimes you have to have hard conversations. Whether it's a poor performance review or a heated disagreement over the best way forward on a project, emotions can run high. If we know the conversation is going to be emotional or recognize that it's becoming that way during a call, we've found the best approach is to agree to address it in a different format. We try to save the really emotional topics for face-to-face discussions (this includes any performance review, good or bad). If that's not possible and the conversation must take place virtually, we lay out ground rules ahead of time. For example, we advise people to ask permission before giving hard feedback. A simple "Are you mentally ready to receive feedback?" can go a long way toward making the conversation go more smoothly.

Hopefully by now you've realized how your culture can and should impact how you conduct conference calls and virtual meetings. As the main way virtual employees interact with one another, conference calls can truly make or break your success in creating a strong virtual culture. Thinking through how they will work for your company is an important task that should be treated with a lot of care and consideration.

Choose Your Tools Wisely

Centric's business model has always relied on regular communication and collaboration, so the lack of affordable tools allowing direct voice-to-voice communication was a meaningful hurdle to overcome 20 years ago when the company started.

Early on our approach to conference calls involved making a coordinated set of three-way calls on cell phones until everyone was joined in a chain. The process was initiated with an email to all participants identifying a list of everyone and the order in which they were to be joined to the call. Everyone had to be ready on time so that when they were called by the person before them on the list, they could answer and continue the chain.

After we managed to connect everyone, most of our conference calls were very effective, although inefficient by today's standards. Keep in mind that the quality of cell service has radically improved over the past 20 years—our most common issue was when someone in the middle of the phone chain would drop their call, suddenly disconnecting half of the participants. A flurry of texts and emails would help us figure out where the chain was broken so we could reconnect and try to pick up where we left off.

Needless to say, our calls are shorter today, and we accomplish much more in an hourlong call than we did 20 years ago. However, as frustrating as our earlier process sounds, we laughed and joked about it more than we complained, and not a day passes that we don't appreciate tools like Microsoft Teams and how easy it is now to collaborate.

—Jeff L., Cincinnati, Ohio

We've been operating virtually for 20 years. Thankfully, the tools we use to connect virtually have steadily improved. We've always made it work, but as you can tell from Jeff's story, our virtual work was initially less efficient than it would have been in an office. This is no longer the case—it's now possible to seamlessly collaborate with anyone anywhere in the world.

That said, if you are going to operate virtually, you have to think through what tools you'll rely upon (we take a deep dive on this in chapter 9). Some options facilitate collaboration better than others. For instance, we recently switched to Microsoft Teams, a collaboration suite of tools for video conferencing, chatting, and shared workspaces, and it has greatly increased our productivity. You also need to be prepared to regularly explore your options—you never know when a better tool will become available.

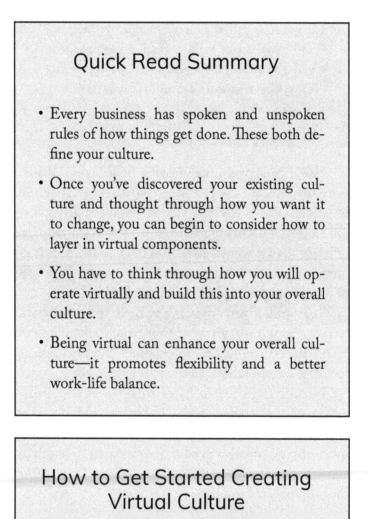

Quick Read Summary

- Every business has spoken and unspoken rules of how things get done. These both define your culture.

- Once you've discovered your existing culture and thought through how you want it to change, you can begin to consider how to layer in virtual components.

- You have to think through how you will operate virtually and build this into your overall culture.

- Being virtual can enhance your overall culture—it promotes flexibility and a better work-life balance.

How to Get Started Creating Virtual Culture

- You have to do the hard work of discovering and redefining what your culture is today. Do this by determining your company's "why," as well as its unwritten rules, traditions, operating philosophies, who gets hired and promoted, and how employees are rewarded.

- Once you have discovered your core culture, layer in virtual components that will enhance and improve your core culture.

- As you extend your culture to virtual workers, consider how you will conduct calls, when people need to be available for work, and what tools you will need to enhance collaboration.

Challenges You Will Encounter

- If your company currently operates 100 percent in-office, there may be reluctance to allow virtual work. Virtual efforts can fail if company leaders shackle employees with rigid rules.

- You need to allow time to get your footing operating virtually. Operations will be clunky at first.

3

The Most Important Parts of Your Culture Can't Always Be Taught

We had a recruit in our pipeline who had just graduated from college with an offer from a big consulting firm, but the company rescinded the offer because of a rough economy. I was scheduled to interview him over dinner that week.

I got a call from the recruit prior to the scheduled interview. He said his mom had never heard of a virtual company and she was worried he was going to get bamboozled. He then asked if his mom could come with him to the interview. We were still relatively new, and I was used to having to go to great lengths to convince recruits that we were a real company. "Why not?" I said.

We met at a sit-down restaurant, and they took turns asking me questions. The mom asked me about our company history, how we ran the company, and why we were optimistic about our future. I honestly felt like I was the one being interviewed and regretted not being more prepared. They both were smart and engaging, and I ended up enjoying dinner.

So, I hired him. I know. But hear me out: this was his first job, and he had already been burned by a large corporation. Our virtual model is hard for people to understand, so it was reasonable for him and his mom to be cautious. Still, it has to go down as the strangest recruiting process that I experienced in my career.

Unfortunately, it didn't work out, and we parted company after about a year. While I don't think the helicopter parenting really factored in, I now recommend treating any recruit who brings a blood relative to an interview with caution.

—Dave R., Ann Arbor, Michigan

We have a lot of stories of hires who ended up being poor matches for our culture. It inevitably becomes painful for everyone, obviously including the employee.

But we've learned a lot along the way, and this mistake is now uncommon.

If you are serious about having a virtual company with excellent culture, you must have the discipline to develop a hiring process that screens for culture matches and for the attributes of successful virtual workers. You can't just hire for skills—that never translates to great culture.

Hire People with Your Culture in Their DNA

"We draft great attitudes . . . We can change skill levels through training. We can't change attitude."
—Herb Kelleher | Southwest Airlines cofounder and former CEO

You know when you fly Southwest that every employee you interact with is going to have a service mindset. They are going to be enjoyable and maybe even entertaining. Southwest has been able to achieve this at scale because it intentionally screens for employees who sincerely want to serve customers. You can't fake that— you're either naturally wired for it or you're not.

Any company that wants a great culture has to hire for both culture fit and skillset. Of course, this is only possible if you know what your culture is and have thought through what type of individuals are successful in your company. What personality traits must employees have inherently baked into their DNA? What traits or skills can you teach? What aspects of your virtual culture are nonnegotiable? What kind of person thrives as a successful remote worker?

In short, you need to think through:

- Aspects of your core culture that CANNOT be taught
- Aspects of your core culture that CAN be taught
- Aspects of your virtual culture that CANNOT be taught
- Aspects of your virtual culture that CAN be taught

Throughout this chapter, I'll walk you through how we've approached these categories so you can apply it to your own company. Parsing apart your culture to come up with these four lists is hard work, but it will ultimately provide a roadmap for who to recruit, how to train employees for your culture, how to evaluate and promote employees, and how to tell it's time to part company with someone who isn't working out.

Aspects of Our Core Culture That CANNOT Be Taught

We screen for and hire people who already have the following aspects of our culture in their DNA; these are things that can't be taught (or can't be taught easily). You either have them or you don't. Keep in mind that our list probably won't—and shouldn't—match yours.

Being kind

Maybe it is our Midwestern roots, but we want employees who are kind. This is a must-have if we want to live our core purpose of creating unmatched experiences for our clients and employees.

Being humble

We have a low-ego culture. We don't like politics. As a consulting company, we advise clients, and clients (rightly) hate when someone is arrogant and condescending. This is why we screen for people who are humble. If someone tends toward arrogance, it's possible to coach them, but this behavior change takes forever and the chance for success is low.

Having integrity

We define integrity as keeping your commitments and always doing the right thing, even when no one is looking. If this isn't already part of someone's personality, it takes too much effort to coach them. Not to mention the consequences can be steep when an employee doesn't demonstrate integrity.

Aspects of Our Core Culture That CAN Be Taught

This is the easiest of the four categories—the things that are vital to your culture but can absolutely be taught to any new employee. In chapter 5, we'll explain how we teach our culture. For now, here are a few examples of the teachable parts of our culture.

How to live a balanced lifestyle

For many years, I worked for a large consulting firm and traveled Monday through Thursday every week. My approach was to stay at the client site until my to-do list was done for that day (whether it was 7 p.m. or 10 p.m.). After walking out of the client's doors, I would not think about their project challenges until the next day. I relieved stress by separating work and life activities.

My son is a really good athlete, but baseball was never his strong suit. To give you an idea, he would typically miss pitches by about two feet. Until I joined Centric.

My schedule became more flexible, and I worked a fair amount from home. This allowed me to be an assistant coach on my son's sports teams, which I had never been able to do in the past. My son and I began at-home batting practice in the afternoons before games. Every week, he missed my first 10 pitches, but after about 60, he would be dialed in and primed to play his best.

Although I may have needed to catch up on some work later that evening or take a quick phone call during batting practice, spending time with my son and watching him succeed was special. Now that we are older and he is through most of his intense competitions, I am grateful to have been able to balance work and life to capture some of life's most precious memories.

—Chris S., Cincinnati, Ohio

We have had to teach many new hires to find better balance between work and their life outside of work. Many of the people we've hired from the big international consulting firms have had to go through a "detox" as they learn that we don't work nonstop with high-hour weeks and we absolutely take vacation.

How to deliver for clients

We hire people who are already great at their craft. What we sometimes have to teach is our client delivery mindset. We take our commitment to our clients to a whole different level, delivering on our commitments

100 percent of the time. Our consultants are always happy to help out, whether that means lending their expertise when another client team gets in a bind, worrying about getting the job done as if it were their own company, or simply treating clients like friends.

How to innovate

As a tech company, we have to be great at innovation. It is both a mindset and a process. Every single person naturally has great ideas, but most new recruits don't understand how to test and cultivate them. Employees going through our innovation program learn concepts like Human-Centered Design and Lean Startup—innovation methodologies that are unlike any processes they've used before. If you give your team an innovation platform and process that allows their ideas to flourish, you will be blown away at the creativity and ROI your company can achieve from innovation.

How to be vulnerable

Early in my consulting career, I traveled a lot cross-country. One afternoon when I landed, I quickly stood up in the third row, put my computer bag over my shoulder, and raced off the plane when the doors opened. When I was a couple of steps down the aisle, I was yanked backward and saw an older man come flying toward me. I looked down and saw my computer bag zipper had hooked on the man's pants zipper! Without thinking, I knelt down in the aisle while everyone crowded around me, wondering why we weren't moving. The older man and his wife were German and were saying plenty of heated things. Under pressure, I had forgotten how to speak German, but I could still recognize all the unflattering swear words they were yelling. I looked up at the man and gave him a helpless expression as I proceeded to carefully unhook the zippers. My hands were shaking, and my forehead was sweating as if I were playing a game of Operation. Others were offering to help after the flight attendant announced we had an issue at the front of the plane. The German language progressively got angrier. And then suddenly, I got it! As I stood up, I finally found my German words to say, "I am sorry and thank you for your patience. Enjoy the rest of your trip." They were shocked that I spoke German, and I ran as fast as I could off the plane.

—Wes R., Seattle, Washington

The ability to be vulnerable is critical to building relationships and culture. I personally have struggled with learning how to model vulnerability as a leader. It was painful at first, but over time it's become easier. (More on the value of vulnerability in chapter 6.)

To help employees become comfortable with vulnerability, we open our culture training with an exercise where we ask them to share one of their most embarrassing moments (like the one above). The exercise helps teach everyone that it's okay to show weakness and that we have a safe environment where sharing what you don't know helps all improve and make better decisions. It's a research-backed approach: the anticipation of embarrassment inhibits creativity, so sharing a story gets that out of the way and helps us connect with one another on a human level.[1]

Aspects of Our Virtual Culture That CANNOT Be Taught

Virtual employees must have certain traits to be successful. Again, these are things that cannot be taught. They include:

A genuine interest in helping people

Relationship building is critical in a virtual organization but can be difficult when you're not in a physical office. How a candidate builds relationships and under what motivation can tell us a lot about whether they'll be a good fit for our culture. We've found that individuals who do this naturally and from a place of helpfulness and kindness tend to be more successful. They are usually an active force in people's lives, help people and the community on weekends, are easy to talk to, and are easy to trust. This is another trait that is teachable to some extent, but the failure rate is high.

Being collaborative

We have many business entities and are a client-facing business spread out across 12 US offices and India. That alone makes our need for collaboration high. Our existence as a virtual company, however, takes our collaboration requirement to an 11 on a scale of 10. This is why we look for candidates with a natural inclination to be helpful and to collaborate with peers, partners, and clients. Additionally, as a virtual company, all of our employees have to be comfortable connecting and working with people from all over and in different modes of remote communication.

Being enjoyable to be around

Great personalities can't be taught. We hire recruits with natural charisma and personality because it is much easier to build a relationship with someone virtually when they are engaging and fun.

Aspects of Our Virtual Culture That CAN Be Taught

Whether you're considering letting some team members start to work remotely or building a totally remote team, you may have to coach virtual employees a bit to get them up to speed on some essential remote-work skills. Teachable parts of Centric's virtual culture include:

Working from home

Although most everyone can learn to work virtually, many people struggle at first. (Tips are covered in chapter 10). But once they get the hang of it, most employees actually prefer working virtually to being stuck in an office.

> I was elated to be back in the consulting world, and I feverishly spent my first day at Centric creating the plan for launching the Charlotte team. I received a handful of emails and phone calls welcoming me to the firm, and I felt honored to be part of such a caring, high-performing organization. My second day was filled with the same level of excitement and energy, but fewer messages. By day three, my excitement was waning. Had I made a terrible mistake?
>
> Upon reflection, I discovered that I felt alone and isolated—I spent my day staring at the same four walls. I realized I had no idea what it meant to work remotely. Missing the casual interactions and periodic breaks that are commonplace to an office environment, I knew I had to find a way to make this working remote thing work for me.
>
> First, I tried spending a few days a week working from a coffee shop. The noise and energy were a welcome change from the solitude of

my home office and actually improved my productivity—for a period of time. While great for independent work, the coffee shop was not so ideal for client calls or to work collaboratively with my Centric colleagues on client proposals.

Through trial and error, I found I was able to maximize my productivity and the enjoyment I found in my work by aligning where I work with what I am working on and changing locations once or twice a day. Despite the time commuting between locations, this actually helps me to produce a higher-quality product.

Now that I've found a system that works for me, I have serious concerns about my ability to ever go back to an office-based structure.

—TJ F., Charlotte, North Carolina

Workday balance

So many people have been conditioned with the mindset that they have to be at a desk from eight to five, and they feel guilty if they are doing a nonwork activity during those hours. We have to help most new employees unlearn this and to feel it's okay to break the normal workday routine so long as they are meeting their work obligations and client expectations. That said, it's also important for remote workers to communicate their schedules with their team members.

Virtual meeting protocol

From the previous chapter, you know how important virtual meetings are to a remote company. New employees can quickly model behavior after seeing how just one or two calls are conducted.

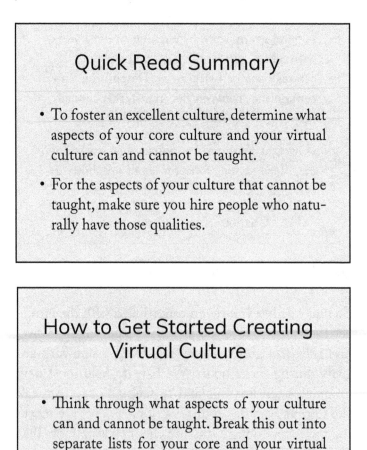

Quick Read Summary

- To foster an excellent culture, determine what aspects of your core culture and your virtual culture can and cannot be taught.

- For the aspects of your culture that cannot be taught, make sure you hire people who naturally have those qualities.

How to Get Started Creating Virtual Culture

- Think through what aspects of your culture can and cannot be taught. Break this out into separate lists for your core and your virtual cultures. Use this list to guide your screening questions and hiring decisions.

Challenges You Will Encounter

- Listing employee traits and skills that can and cannot be taught is difficult work, requiring you to have a firm grasp on your culture and how it applies to virtual workers

4

How to Hire Culture Amplifiers and Virtual Work Superstars

I had reached out to a candidate to set up an interview. He told me he was going to be on vacation but was open to doing the call. I said we were flexible and could wait, but he really wanted to move forward. When I called him at the agreed-upon time, there was a lot of commotion going on around him. I couldn't figure out what was happening, but there was music and kids screaming, and he was clearly distracted. Not far into the interview, the call dropped. When I tried to call him back, it went straight to voicemail.

He called me back hours later and solved the
mystery for me: He had been in line for the
Tower of Terror at Disney World with his kids!
When they moved up in the line, he had lost
mobile coverage.

This was obviously not the best choice of venue
to conduct an interview.

—Fiona F., Seattle, Washington

When we recruit, determining whether candidates
align with our values and culture is the most critical
part of our interview process, which is why we only
spend about 50 percent of the time discussing skill
qualifications. We spend the rest of the interview making sure the person has our core culture traits that can't
be taught, the ones we discussed in the previous chapter.

Of course, hiring for culture fit doesn't mean we're
looking to hire people who act, think, and look exactly
alike. A wide diversity of backgrounds, ideas, opinions,
and viewpoints is ideal. What we do want alignment
on is our value system—we want people who are collaborative, kind, have a genuine interest in helping people, and are enjoyable to be around.

Being a virtual company means much of our recruiting process is also completed virtually. This, of
course, comes with unique challenges. This chapter details how we overcome these challenges and maintain a
focus on hiring for culture.

The Recruiting Process

There is nothing overtly unusual about our recruiting process. What is unique, however, is that we screen for culture nearly every step of the way.

First, we conduct a prescreen in which a recruiter has an initial call with the candidate. They cover an overview of Centric and the role and have a high-level conversation around the candidate's technical and functional skills as compared to the job requirements and salary expectations. The recruiter will also initially assess whether the person is a culture fit.

Next, we schedule a skillset screen, an in-depth call to assess if the candidate has the skills needed to do the job. For technical roles, this could mean a test followed by a detailed phone interview. We also continue screening for culture.

The final step is an in-depth interview, usually with multiple people. Each interviewer drills down into a specific area of the job responsibilities while also trying to determine if the person is a culture fit. If we sense for any reason that the person might not be a fit (what we call yellow flags, which you'll learn about later), we set up additional interviews to dive into areas of concern.

Screening for Culture Fit

We continue to experiment with the latest recruitment tools like behavioral interviewing and personality profiling tests. But we've been screening for culture for 20 years and have found a low-tech, low-cost approach can be just as effective.

To recruit for culture fit, you need to know the traits required to be successful in your culture (see chapter 2) and screen for these during interviews. Here's how we do this at Centric.

We tell stories!

Similar to the anecdotes in this book, we share stories so candidates understand what our culture is all about, what we value, and how we get work done. These stories bring our company to life. If a candidate doesn't get excited about our culture, we know they won't stick around. This also helps some candidates self-select out, knowing we aren't for them.

We ask situational questions

This helps us understand a candidate's thought processes and beliefs and whether they have our cultural DNA in them. For example, we might ask: "Talk to me about the last time you made a big mistake. Did you tell your manager? Did you tell the client? If you did tell, how did you do it?" The candidate's answer usually tells us whether they embody our core cultural values.

We engage our culture protectors

We have candidates interview with multiple Centric employees who we consider to be culture stewards.

If someone doesn't feel like the candidate is a culture match, we make sure the next interviewer can dig deeper into areas of concern.

We commit the time

Recruiting isn't just the job of our recruiters. Our leadership invests a lot of time with candidates, too, helping us determine whether the person is a fit for Centric (and vice versa). Candidates value this investment because it illustrates our commitment to them as a recruit. While this does lengthen the recruiting process, which can be frustrating to some, we've found that the recruits who value our culture are more than willing to take a little extra time or schedule an additional interview.

We introduce candidates to the team

During a team interview, candidates meet with three or more Centric people representing diverse backgrounds, thinking styles, and roles. The candidate gets a better feel for how the team interacts, and we get to see how the candidate acts and reacts in a small group setting.

Knowing When to Dig Deeper

When we are assessing a candidate, we'll often see things that may indicate the person isn't a culture fit.

We call these red flags and yellow flags. The designation helps us know when it's worth our time to dig in and when we should pass on the candidate.

Red flags

A red flag tells us the candidate has a quality in direct opposition to one of our core culture traits. This is usually obvious. For example, if the candidate is overly preoccupied with what their title would be, we know they aren't a fit and they don't make it past the screening interview. That is why we look at culture fit from the very beginning—it saves us a lot of time and money the earlier we can figure out the person won't work out.

Yellow flags

Yellow flags are more subtle. If we see one, we really dig into the area of concern. Yes, it slows down our hiring process. Yes, it can be frustrating to a candidate. But outweighing these concerns is our desire to keep our culture intact and to hire people for life. Slowing down ultimately benefits the candidate, too. If we were to hire them and they weren't a culture fit, they would struggle in our environment and eventually leave.

> We received a referral and had the opportunity to grow our senior leadership team. Things were great during the first round of interviews with leadership. The candidate said all of the "right things." We were sold!

It was so tempting to shortcut our process. Not having an office sometimes draws our interviews out into multiple rounds over a couple of weeks, and we needed help ASAP to support our rapid growth. But we stuck with our process and set up a lunch without leadership.

This is when we saw a yellow flag. Maybe even orange. The tone was different this time. The team felt like the person wasn't really listening to them and didn't try to connect with them. We realized we needed to dive in deeper.

Our next step was to set up additional conversations to really assess the candidate on our core values, especially around our concern over whether they could be a humble leader. We also arranged to have the candidate work with us as a team on a deliverable. That's when the yellow flag turned red. Natural collaboration can sound like a soft skill, but when you are working with a team, it's immediately apparent whether someone has it. The person had strong opinions about content and format and a hierarchy of how decisions should be made. We knew we should pass.

Was this an expensive "interview"? Maybe. But it remains one of our greatest happy stories about slowing down the recruitment process. If we would have plowed forward, we would have lost our team's enthusiasm for a new senior member, and we would have ultimately put someone in a place where they wouldn't be successful.

After this experience, we made a couple of permanent changes to how we interviewed. We made the team lunch without leadership an essential part of our interview process and inserted small ways to test collaboration abilities. Ultimately, who we hire shows how committed we are to our core values, which reinforces their importance with each team member in a way that pays dividends every day.

—Paul H., St. Louis, Missouri

In-Person or Virtual Interviews?

Early on, when we were still figuring out our business model, we had a candidate who we interviewed virtually but hadn't been able to meet face-to-face. He was a great fit and would be subcontracting to us, so we took the chance of bringing him on without meeting him in person. We thought the risk was small.

I arranged to meet him at a coffee shop an hour before he would start at the client site. I spotted him from across the room and was relieved to see he had a professional appearance. I sat down and introduced myself. When he spoke, I recoiled. He had the worst breath I had ever smelled.

My mind was racing. Do I tell him? How do I tell him? Does Starbucks sell mouthwash? I mustered up the courage and told him in the most humane and nicest way possible. He was mortified and turned red. We finished the conversation and we both quickly, awkwardly left. After telling him, he was able to better prepare before showing up to meet a new client.

—Larry E., Columbus, Ohio

This is an unusual example of something you can't determine through virtual interviews. While you can absolutely make solid hiring decisions using only phone and video calls—and we do in a number of situations—face-to-face meetings have some advantages, as illustrated in the story above.

For most of our roles, we believe we can evaluate about 90 percent of our hiring criteria through a combination of phone and video calls. That final 10 percent consists of soft skills that are difficult to assess without meeting someone in person. The subtle personality traits that don't come across in a virtual call include:

- How does the candidate act in a social setting with other people? Do they look the person in the eye? Are they kind to the greeting staff or waitstaff? Do they pick up on social cues? How do they handle conflict with others, like a bumped chair or incorrect lunch order?

- How does the person carry themselves when they walk in the room? Do they have a great professional edge about them? Do they have a quiet confidence, or are they awkward?

- If you're interviewing them in a restaurant, do they focus on you, or are they distracted watching other people? Are they repeatedly checking their watch?

By meeting someone in person, you get a holistic feel for their body language that doesn't come through on a video call. We have also found candidates to be less vulnerable over a phone or video call, whereas in person, you can't really hide. Your personality is more completely on display.

Centric is a consulting firm, so most of our employees interact with clients in person at some point. The bar is really high for being skilled in social interactions. This is why we continue to require in-person interviews for any role that requires a high degree of in-person interaction, collaboration among many groups of people, and mastery of soft skills.

We've also found that some candidates need the reassurance that comes from a face-to-face interview. Although virtual companies are becoming more common, many recruits are still skeptical when they can't go to an office building. Meeting in person gives candidates an additional level of confidence to accept the offer.

When Virtual Interviews Are Sufficient

In the gig world, everyone is increasingly collaborating online and never meeting in person. In fact, we know of many companies that never require in-person interviews. In other words, a face-to-face interview isn't always necessary. Here's when we skip it:

- When the person will be interacting with us 100 percent virtually. We have sourcing recruiters whose job is completely remote. We've hired for these roles without an in-person interview and haven't regretted it yet.

- When the role doesn't require advanced social skills. When less in-person interaction is needed, we often skip the face-to-face time.

- When the role is temporary. When we're hiring someone who isn't coming on board full time, we often take the risk of making a decision based on a video or phone call.

The cultural traits that are critical for success in your company will also provide some guidance on whether or not you need in-person interviews. Our culture emphasizes how we interact with one another and with clients, so in-person interviews are the norm rather than the exception. Your company might be different, and a phone call may be enough to tell you whether a candidate is a culture match.

Sticking to Your Guns

This is the true test of your commitment to culture as a leader: do you stick to your guns and make sure that every person you hire is a culture fit with no exceptions? This is harder than it may seem—you will likely encounter tremendous pressure to shortcut the screening process or accept a less-than-perfect match. It will be especially tempting when you have a customer need that has to be filled tomorrow. But shortcutting the process is never a good idea. For instance, we often run into geniuses who are hard to work with or sales rainmakers who won't collaborate. Only by going through every step of our process do we uncover these fatal flaws.

We've learned that as soon as you start to compromise and hire people who aren't a fit, your culture starts to deteriorate and heads in the direction of no return. The tradeoff is slower growth and the pain of waiting for someone who is a good match. But the wait is well worth the price for an outstanding culture.

When you take your time during the recruitment process to ensure candidates are a culture match, you will likely find turnover decreases. Low turnover is good for general morale. It also benefits the bottom line: it costs companies one-third of a worker's salary to hire a replacement, not to mention the productivity costs of the recruitment activities and the extra tasks added to your existing employees' workloads.[1]

Our turnover hovers around 7 percent, and when we make an offer, we have a 98 percent acceptance rate. We haven't done the math, but we're confident that retaining top talent is worth the extra upfront recruitment effort.

When a Mismatch Sneaks Through

Employee referrals for potential recruits are the lifeblood of a company like Centric that prides itself on hiring people who are going to enhance our culture. Who better than someone who already works at Centric to understand what it takes to be successful here?

When considering a referral, we once took a shortcut to our normal hiring process and also neglected to vet how well the referring employee knew the candidate. You know where this is headed.

Here are just a few of the oddities the new hire exhibited in the first month. During onboarding, he didn't look at the person trying to talk him through the material. Instead, he spent the whole time reading and texting on his phone. In our culture training, he referred to the loaded gun in his car. On his first project, he kept talking about how "hot" his wife was. He would get up during meetings multiple times and adjust the thermostat to his liking without asking anyone else how they felt. He would type on his keyboard so loudly it was like he was giving a piano recital.

We obviously had to part ways (and never shortcut our recruitment process again).

—Matt H., Cincinnati, Ohio

The example in the story above is extreme, but you're bound to make mistakes, missing cues that someone is a poor fit. This usually happens when we rush through our process or skip important steps. When we find we've hired someone who doesn't embody our culture, two things happen:

- We look at what we missed throughout recruitment. Did we skip a step in the process? Do we need to fix a hole in our process? There is almost always an improvement that can be made.

- If the person is clearly not a culture fit and we can't fix it, we try to act quickly and nicely part ways. Otherwise, the person can bring down the morale of the entire team, and the performance of the team suffers greatly. Everyone knows they are a bad match, and they'll be looking to you to step up and fix it.

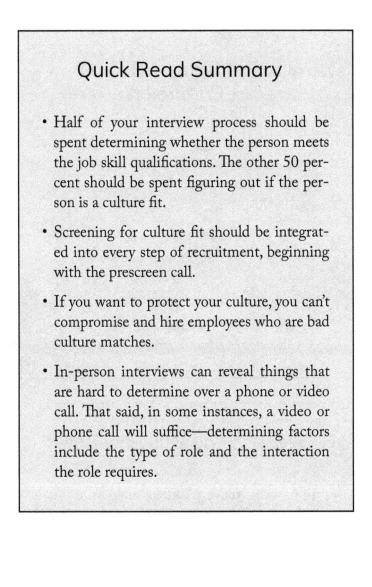

Quick Read Summary

• Half of your interview process should be spent determining whether the person meets the job skill qualifications. The other 50 percent should be spent figuring out if the person is a culture fit.

• Screening for culture fit should be integrated into every step of recruitment, beginning with the prescreen call.

• If you want to protect your culture, you can't compromise and hire employees who are bad culture matches.

• In-person interviews can reveal things that are hard to determine over a phone or video call. That said, in some instances, a video or phone call will suffice—determining factors include the type of role and the interaction the role requires.

How to Get Started Recruiting for Culture Fit

• Develop a recruiting process that screens for culture fit during every step. Include people in the recruiting process who really understand your culture.

• Develop protocol for knowing when to dig deeper and knowing when to pass on a candidate.

• Develop protocol for when face-to-face interviews will be required and when a phone or video interview will suffice.

Challenges You Will Encounter

• The commitment to never compromise in hiring for culture fit is difficult. Your business could grow slower, and there will be tremendous temptation to speed up the process.

5

Scaling Your Culture with a Cultural Training Program

Before I went to Centric's new employee orientation, I had heard it was a blast. And it was definitely was! Every company I've worked for does an orientation, but Centric takes it a step further and gives new employees an enthusiastic welcome and introduction to their awesome culture. My favorite part of the experience was making a race car out of LEGOs! Need I say more?

But more importantly, hearing Centric's leaders describe the type of people the company looks for made me feel really comfortable with my choice to come on board. For the first time, I felt like I'm where I should have been all along. It was such a positive experience that made me realize I'm working for an amazing company that really believes in investing in their people from day one. It showed me I wasn't just employee number "99999999." It was more like, "James, welcome to Centric, let's go to Chicago and we'll introduce you to a cool company!"

—James T., Columbus, Ohio

It's easy to maintain company culture when you're small. In the early days of Centric, we loved everyone we worked with and even knew everyone's spouses and kids. But we also knew we had to grow to keep all of the great, highly motivated people at our company.

When we hit that growth period and began rapidly adding new employees, we started to see cracks in our culture. A growing list of situations weren't handled the way we would have liked. As a leadership team, we could no longer spend time with every employee to teach them our value system and our culture. Being virtual compounded the problem.

To ensure the culture we loved remained intact as we grew, we developed an in-depth culture curriculum. This has expanded over the years and is now a yearlong process, with a more intensive track for company leaders (we'll share more details later in this chapter).

Surprisingly, we're in the minority in training our employees specifically on culture. Although the busi-

ness world loves to wax poetic about culture, 61 percent
of companies fail to even mention the topic in employee onboarding sessions.[1]

It's almost too obvious to say, but if you want great
culture, you have to actually tell your employees what
your culture is and what it means to live up to it. Training everyone on your culture also ensures that your clients and business partners have a consistent experience
that aligns with your vision for your company. This is
precisely the point of our culture curriculum, and it sets
employees up for success from day one.

Welcome to the Couch

As we were serving our first major client, we
worked out of several apartments with rent-
to-own furniture. The main apartment where
we gathered had our favorite couch where we
spent countless hours debating our vision for
the company. When the project ended, I took
the couch and put it in my home office.

My wife hated the couch. It was ugly when it
was brand new. Over the years, my four boys
jumped on it so much that the springs became
shot. If you sat in the couch, you sank to the
ground.

When we were developing our new-hire orientation, we remembered back to our days
dreaming up our culture sitting on that couch.

We thought the couch was a perfect reminder of where we had come from, a symbol of our humble roots, like the garage that Apple was founded in.

We decided to bring the couch on stage for an all-company meeting. I was leaving for an early morning trip and had forgotten that I was supposed to put the couch in my garage to be picked up by movers. It was the middle of February in Ohio, and the only way to get it to the garage was going through the back door and trudging through the snowed-in backyard—definitely a two-person job. I tiptoed into my bedroom and gingerly woke my wife, saying, "Honey, I love you a lot."

As we were carrying the couch through snow at 5 a.m., my wife only said one seething sentence through her gritted teeth: "This is a one-way trip."

—Larry E., Columbus, Ohio

Our culture training begins with a one-day course for new employees. The experience couldn't be further from a boring recitation of an HR manual. It's a fun, high-energy day that brings our culture to life. We sing, we do stupid human tricks, we tell embarrassing stories about ourselves, and we laugh a lot. The participant evaluations are all 9s and 10s on a scale of 10.

The training is a big investment. We fly everyone into one of the cities where we operate and make the commitment to have our top leaders run each session. We want employees to hear about our culture and learn to live it directly from our founders and senior leaders.

Throughout the day, we teach new employees about our culture and the key traits that can and can't be taught (remember this from chapter 2?). Among other activities, we:

- Have teams build and race LEGO cars to teach our approach to collaborative innovation

- Have teams develop and perform songs where each team member contributes their own beat to show how we approach and value diversity

- Tell stories about our failures and successes to teach situational awareness and how to apply our culture traits when employees encounter similar situations

- Have new employees draw and describe their life to illustrate what it means to them to be balanced

While our learning activities are always evolving, the lessons employees learn during this culture orientation are reinforced through their entire first year at Centric with virtual sessions with leadership and online courses on topics like how to deliver an unmatched customer and employee experience. Employees complete about 90 percent of the training virtually at their own pace on a cloud-based tool; the remaining 10 percent requires a high degree of collaboration. For that, we bring people together.

This mix of virtual and in-person training is impactful. A 2019 new employee onboarding study shows employees prefer blended learning, in part because it appeals to different learning styles and preferences.[2] LinkedIn found 68 percent of employees like learning at work, while 58 percent learn better at their own pace.[3] Plus, by mixing in some hands-on training activities, we maximize the chances of employees really getting it. Research shows that people can retain 90 percent of information gleaned from experiential learning.[4]

It Starts at the Top

When designing our culture curriculum, we researched companies that maintained their culture as they scaled and spoke with executives at some of those organizations. One secret to success became clear: hire leaders who embody your culture and make sure they infuse it into the area of the business they oversee. If you do this, you can scale your company to thousands of employees and maintain the same culture you had when you were just a handful of people.

Here's how.

Hire carefully

In chapter 4, we discussed the importance of taking your time to hire employees and screen for culture fit.

When you're hiring for a leadership role, you need to follow the same process, but on steroids.

Our interview process for leaders is long and thorough, and we usually look for a trusted third-party reference (one not provided by the candidate) that we source through our own network. If there's even a whisper of a yellow flag, we don't move forward with the candidate. It's a lot of work vetting a leadership candidate, but it's well worth it to avoid hiring a bad fit—replacing a senior executive can cost 200 percent of their salary.[5]

We've found making this mistake can cost us two years in our timeline of growing a new business area. You spend time getting the person up to speed, you spend time giving them the opportunity to be successful when they are struggling, and then you have to spend time conducting a new search for their replacement. That's a lot of hours, not to mention the organizational bandwidth to work through the entire process.

Give leaders a mentor

Employees learn how to live your culture by watching your leaders. If your leaders don't get it, there's no hope for everyone else. Official leader mentorship programs can help. According to a survey of CEOs, 71 percent found having a mentor improved business performance, 69 percent said it helped them make better decisions, and 84 percent said their mentor helped them quickly learn the ropes in their role.[6]

When we hire a new leader to start a business group, we pair them with a senior executive who mentors them for their first two years on the job. One of the mentor's key responsibilities is to provide guidance on executing and living our culture. They gently guide the new leader as they infuse our culture into the new business group. For example, both leaders will screen and interview all candidates for that business unit and compare notes until the new leader is self-sufficient in selecting candidates who align with our values and culture.

Provide formalized leadership development

Centric's unmatched experience mindset has profoundly shaped the leadership skills I developed earlier in my career. What really put it all together for me was my involvement in our leadership development program.

One of the best experiences within the program was a workshop where we reviewed a series of case studies to think through how we could translate our innate, natural tendencies into deliberate actions to shape and advance the organization. The company's top leadership participated, helping us connect the dots and providing context around how it all related back to our core values.

Going through this exercise helped me correlate Centric's unmatched culture with concrete actions I could take to grow my contribution as a leader. Most importantly, it showed me how I could be myself to contribute to our culture and success.

—Sean N., Chicago, Illinois

Any investment that makes your leaders stronger and more attuned to your culture will have a major ROI. After all, leaders are the gatekeepers for your culture, and companies with strong culture are 1.5 times likelier to report revenue growth of over 15 percent.[7]

There is a sea of leadership training programs out there to choose from. Wading through them feels a little like drowning. For example, the Korn Ferry Global Competency Framework lists 67 leadership competencies.[8] The harsh truth is if you care about your culture and want your leaders to support, nurture, and reinforce it, you may need to build your own program.

That's what we did. Our leadership development program teaches new leaders to lead the Centric way, showing them how to anchor their decision-making process to our core values. The program is a never-ending process rooted in continuous learning and improvement. The basic structure involves:

Discovery. New leaders complete a self-assessment against the key Centric leadership traits. One of our leadership traits is to radiate trust, which means we expect our leaders to keep commitments, whether small or large, earn the trust and respect of others by honoring confidences, and always match their deeds with their words.

The leader then goes through a 360-degree feedback process to receive input from everyone they work with. We assign them a leadership coach who helps the leader create a tailored development plan to close the gap that inevitably exists between the reviewers' feedback on the competencies they need to work on and the leader's self-assessment.

Journey. Next, the leader begins executing on the development plan they created with their leadership coach. Their customized path can involve external or internal training and rotating through roles to gain a specific exposure or mentorship by a particular leader. Throughout this process, the leader continues to work with their coach and direct supervisor to assess their progress and course correct as needed.

Centric case study training. New leaders participate in a one-day training course that exposes them to the key leadership traits we expect them to exercise to sustain our culture. Case studies provide real-life examples of times we have failed to lead with these traits. The case studies are based on intentionally challenging realistic, nuanced scenarios and are designed specifically to give our new batch of leaders a solid understanding of how to lead within our culture and value system.

Beyond driving profits, exceptional leaders are also the best chance you have for ensuring your culture survives over the years and through the generations. We view our significant investment in our customized leadership program as insurance against culture erosion as we grow and as the next generation of leaders takes the helm.

Cultural Ambassadors

Although the fate of your culture rests on the shoulders of your leaders, all employees are influencers of culture—they live it out every day. And employees at all levels can be invaluable resources in keeping your culture strong. This was the reasoning behind Centric's newly implemented cultural ambassador program, designed to assist company leaders in making sure our culture reaches every part of the business. Each operating group appoints a cultural ambassador—someone the group feels upholds the company's values and beliefs. There are no other real qualifications beyond that; our cultural ambassadors come from diverse backgrounds and roles. They're responsible for:

- Promoting our core value of greater good by identifying local charities for Centric to support

- Promoting our core value of innovation by organizing an internal hackathon

- Being a confidential sounding board for situations where employees feel we are not living up to our culture

- Addressing culture concerns that are identified in our employee satisfaction surveys

- Providing feedback on important decisions such as strategy or HR policies that may impact our culture

No matter how good your employees are, they can't read your mind. Your culture will never survive if you don't take the time to teach new employees about it and show your leaders how to keep your culture intact as the company grows.

Quick Read Summary

- Our culture started to crack as we scaled. Realizing how central culture is to our success, we developed our own culture curriculum and train every new employee on it.

- Employees complete about 90 percent of our training virtually through cloud-based tools. The other 10 percent—any part of the curriculum that requires a high degree of collaboration—is done in person.

- The key to scaling your culture lies in leadership. Specifically, you must hire leaders who embody your culture and train them to lead in a way that aligns with your culture and values.

- We implemented a cultural ambassador system to help leaders maintain culture across different departments.

How to Get Started Communicating Your Culture

- Develop a cultural training program for educating all new employees.

- Hire leaders who are a strong culture fit. Develop leadership training to ensure they know how to lead with your culture.

- Develop a cultural ambassador program in each of your operating groups that guides the development of your culture and maintains it across the entire company.

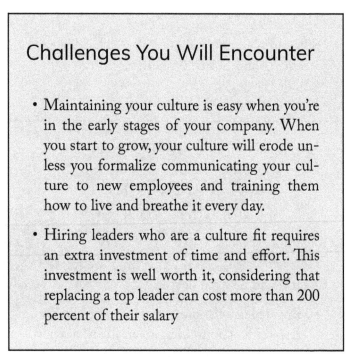

Challenges You Will Encounter

- Maintaining your culture is easy when you're in the early stages of your company. When you start to grow, your culture will erode unless you formalize communicating your culture to new employees and training them how to live and breathe it every day.

- Hiring leaders who are a culture fit requires an extra investment of time and effort. This investment is well worth it, considering that replacing a top leader can cost more than 200 percent of their salary

6

Separate but Connected: How to Build Strong Virtual Relationships

We had been working on a successful client project for three years, our joint team spread across four different cities. Throughout all that time, we never met face-to-face, but we still built strong relationships founded on trust. We shared many small moments over the years, like the countless times my four dogs would chime in at the precise moment when a decision was to be made. This happened so often, we would stop before making a decision to ask the dogs their opinion. The day we finally met felt in some way like a family reunion, with hugs and smiles as we eagerly shared pictures of all the things we had talked about over the years.

—Cindy S., Providence, Rhode Island

***

It can be so comforting to walk into a room and have people greet you with your name and a smile (think "Norm!" from the TV show *Cheers*). But can you create this same feeling in a virtual company that does most of its business via conference calls? We have found the answer to be a wholehearted "yes."

I've worked in our internal operational area for eight years, and I've been on countless leadership calls with more than 75 participants. I (and many others) can almost always recognize who someone is simply by their voice.

Getting to this level of familiarity requires intentional mental effort. It is critical to be an active listener. I have found being ultra-focused on learning the sound of people's voices allows me to learn their name and so much more. Many other leaders from the C-suite on down have done the same thing. It makes such an impact to jump on a phone call, add a comment, and have another company leader say, "Kevin, thanks for sharing . . ." without me having to ever introduce myself.

This small thing makes our conference calls feel like a place you want to go . . . where everybody knows your name, and they're always glad you came.

—Kevin S., Dayton, Ohio

As these stories illustrate, it is possible to build strong relationships and never meet face-to-face—it just happens through different communication channels. But the foundation is the same: you build trust through repeated, meaningful interactions and by connecting on a personal level.

Virtual interactions can take place over the phone, video calls, conference calls, email, and collaboration tools. To build deep relationships over these mediums, however, does take deliberate effort. The necessary ingredients include vulnerability, bringing your whole self to work, taking time to nurture personal relationships, and knowing how to resolve conflict when it arises.

Braving a Little Vulnerability

When we show up as our true selves, openly admitting flaws, knowledge gaps, fears, and mistakes, we're being vulnerable. Vulnerability is the secret ingredient and shortest route to building any strong, collaborative relationship, whether your relationship is strictly virtual or in person. Like most things human, it comes down to neuroscience: when we're vulnerable, we stimulate oxytocin production in others, which increases trust and empathy and fuels cooperation.[1]

In *The Culture Code: The Secrets of Highly Successful Groups*, author Daniel Coyle uses the following quote from Jeffrey Polzer, an organizational behavior professor at Harvard, to describe vulnerability and its importance to cementing collaborative work teams:

> **"People tend to think of vulnerability in a touchy-feely way, but that's not what's happening. . . . It's about sending a really clear signal that you have weaknesses, that you could use help. And if the behavior becomes a model for others, then you can set the insecurities aside and get to work, start to trust each other and help each other."**
> **—Jeffrey Polzer**

At Centric, we encourage employees to take time for real, vulnerable moments in our interactions, whether they're occurring over group calls, one-on-one interactions, or in-person meetings. Being vulnerable is never easy—it's certainly always been a struggle for me. But if you expect your employees to be vulnerable, you have to model the behavior first. By talking about your own weaknesses, admitting when you're unsure how to proceed, and owning up to mistakes, your employees will feel more at ease doing the same.

I've learned the key to pushing yourself to be vulnerable is to share an extra 10 percent beyond your comfort zone. For example, during the coronavirus pandemic, we began calls by sharing our anxiety and concerns. This was a comforting practice that made us feel less alone during the crisis.

The following exercises can help you access that point of vulnerability and take your relationships, work or otherwise, a little deeper:

Gratitude ping-pong

Gratitude ping-pong is a simple, effective exercise to deepen personal connections and communicate your values. I learned about it from Positive Foundry, a corporate well-being program. You take turns saying something you are grateful for, going back and forth until you reach a set amount of time or run out of things to say.

Color coded depth questions

The color coded depth questions exercise, also from Positive Foundry, has participants ask each other questions that are color coded by vulnerability level. The questions that require the least vulnerability are coded blue: What is your favorite vacation ever? What do you like to do on the weekends? One level deeper is yellow: What's your proudest accomplishment so far? What do you value in a friendship? The questions that require

you to reveal the most about yourself are coded red:
What do you value most in life? What do you wish
more people knew about you? You get to choose what
color question you feel comfortable answering.

Bringing Your Whole Self to Work

Creating connections across cyberspace is tricky,
so I try to find ways to insert my personality in
places where people are not expecting it. Boring
status email? I'll paste a funny meme to the top.
Stodgy PowerPoint presentation? You bet I'm
going to slip a picture of my cats in there.

I am probably best known for my out-of-office
messages. I use these auto-reply emails to share
a little bit of my life with others while putting
a smile on their face. Here are a few of my past
favorites:

Subject: Eating Ice Cream

I'm taking advantage of Centric's generous vacation policy ("self-managed PTO") right now.
That means I'm eating a lot of ice cream and
spending a lot of time on the beach. And it also
means I'm not checking email. After all, we
all know that mixing a smartphone with pea-
nut butter cup ice cream, sand, and saltwater
is a recipe for disaster (but job security for cell
phone repair shops).

Subject: It's Friday, and I'm in love . . .

Like the famous lyrics, I am certainly in love with Fridays during the summertime. So much so that I already started the weekend early. No email for me today . . . see you Monday!

Subject: On the Slopes

I've headed west to catch some powder and will be back April 17. I am hopeful I will return with all limbs intact. During this time, I'm going to do my best to keep my eyes on the mountains and not on my email. If you have an urgent need while I am away, please text me.

—Carmen F., Cleveland, Ohio

***

As a member of the OK Boomer generation, I have learned that cultivating strong relationships virtually can be just as rewarding as those relationships made over sharing a beer after work.

Whenever possible, I attempt to learn a bit about a new team member or colleague by checking out LinkedIn or other sources before our initial conversation. My hope is to find something we have in common so we can quickly move beyond a transactional relationship.

If my brief search doesn't surface common threads, I try to break the ice by using common office humor (like Dilbert) or sharing a personal data point such as, "Looking forward to seeing my daughter this weekend. She lives in Delaware and will be visiting for spring break." Invariably, this leads to a short exchange of personal conversation.

Another practice I use to nurture professional relationships is to periodically reach out just because. It could be an email to share information on a work-related topic of mutual interest, birthday wishes, link to a podcast I think they'd like, congratulations on a promotion, etc. The outreach has to be spontaneous, sincere, and with no expectations of quid pro quo!

—Andy R., Tampa, Florida

Many companies operate under a "nothing personal" philosophy. Communication is kept professional by strictly sticking to the business at hand. At Centric, we encourage the exact opposite. We want everyone to share their personality, to showcase who they are as a person and their interests.

By sharing simple details of your life—the funny thing your pet did this morning, the epic hike you're planning for the weekend, a really great pasta recipe you cooked the other night—others will feel a close personal connection to you. When you have social connections at work, your performance improves.[2] When that happens across entire teams, it's a sure recipe for success.

To that end, we ask everyone to use one-on-one interactions as an opportunity to get to know one another better. Just like any in-person relationship, you have to start with the basics and build from there. We want employees to have a genuine interest in getting to know their teammates, to be curious and learn what matters to the other person—when you understand your coworker or client better, you will have an easier time collaborating on a business problem. You'll be more willing to consider other viewpoints and ideas, and together you'll accomplish great work.

According to *Harvard Business Review*, this psychological approach to encouraging collaboration, where employees learn to listen to one another and treat one another as human beings, is effective. Far more so than paying lip service to collaboration in your mission statement or forcing everyone to work in a noisy open office and hoping collaboration magically happens.[3]

It's important for employees to get to know one another one-on-one, but as I mentioned in an earlier chapter, we also formalize this human-to-human element in our group calls. These always begin with a virtual watercooler chat. This sometimes happens naturally, but often the call's facilitator will plan a question that starts an informal, personal conversation and helps us all get to know one another better. Some examples include:

- If you could live in any sitcom, which one would it be and why?

- Who would you swap places with for a day, and why?

- Fill in the blank: If you really knew me, you'd know _____.

- If you could offer a newborn child only one piece of advice, what would it be?

- What is the greatest piece of advice a parent or mentor has given you?

- If you could choose one hobby that now seems out of your reach either financially or time-wise, what would you take up and why?

- Would you rather see into the future or change your past? Why?

The key is to avoid diving directly into the business agenda. Share personally so everyone feels connected before getting down to the business at hand.

Managing Conflict

Avoiding hard, uncomfortable conversations is human nature. Being in a virtual environment only increases the temptation. But sometimes, hard conversations are necessary, and we want our employees to lean into these discussions.

Conflict is inevitable, and when you are in the middle of it, it's easy to forget that at the end of the conversation you want the relationship to grow. We want everyone to approach conflict resolution with the mindset that maintaining the relationship is priority no. 1, not resolving the business issue at hand.

To help employees feel confident in having the hard talks where the stakes and emotions are high, we provide a training course on the techniques used in the book *Crucial Conversations*. For example, one of the techniques in *Crucial Conversations* is the concept of "making it safe." The idea is you create the right conditions to have the conversation by establishing mutual respect and mutual purpose. By the end of the course, they know how to approach those conversations as an opportunity for an honest human-to-human interaction that ultimately builds a deeper relationship.

Being virtual also means intentions can be misconstrued. You can't see body language and other nonverbal cues over chat or email. In fact, research has shown that people tend to overestimate both their ability to construe a specific tone in emails they're sending and to accurately gauge the tone of emails they receive.[4]

If you sense there might be an issue brewing, take the time for a phone or video call to make sure everything is okay. Let the person know you are double-checking that you're both on the same page. Check the person's temperature to make sure they weren't bothered by something you said. All it takes is picking up the phone and connecting, human to human.

From Virtual to Reality

I began joining our online meetings with my video on, ready to greet colleagues with a hello and a smile, just like I'd do in the real world. Two things became apparent right away. One, I needed to straighten up the bookcase behind my desk (which I did), and two, there was a different energy to these calls. I felt like video helped me develop a deeper connection quicker. I've noticed that people who join my calls are starting to choose to turn on their video as well.

I have so many coworkers I've developed great relationships with virtually. I love the feeling when you finally get to meet in person at a company event. I was recently at one of our in-person events where we train new hires on our culture. After checking in at the opening reception and getting my name tag, I greeted a few Centric friends I've known for years. As I set off to meet and welcome some of the new hires peppered throughout the venue, a guy came up to me sporting a big smile. He extended his hand, saying, "Hey Maurice! It's nice to meet you. It's weird, but I feel like I know you already!" As you might have guessed, this was someone I'd never met in person, but we'd been on a number of video conference calls together. The connection had already been made, and our conversation felt more like we were catching up than meeting face-to-face for the first time.

—Maurice F., Cincinnati, Ohio

I've witnessed hundreds of these virtual reunions when people finally meet in person at one of our all-company meetings. We'll dive into how to optimize in-person meetings in the next chapter, but for now, it's important to note that in-person meetings can cement already-great relationships that have been built in the ether. You don't have to ever meet in person for a culture to be successful, but we have found face-to-face encounters can energize a relationship and make it even stronger.

Quick Read Summary

- You can build strong relationships and never meet face-to-face, but it does take some extra consideration to build those connections over email, phone calls, and collaboration tools.

- Building relationships over virtual channels requires vulnerability, bringing your whole self to work, taking time to foster personal connections, and knowing how to resolve conflict when it arises.

- Research shows that when employees take the time to build personal connections with coworkers through group calls and one-on-one interactions, they collaborate more effectively and see performance improvements.

- Intentions and tone can easily be misconstrued over email and chat. When you're virtual, sometimes you need to pick up the phone to smooth things over or take the temperature of the other person.

How to Get Started Building Deep Virtual Relationships

- When you meet a new coworker, take the time to get to know them before diving into business.

- Even large group calls can offer an opportunity to build connections. Start each virtual meeting with a virtual watercooler where you ask everyone to share something personal.

* Vulnerability is the shortcut to fostering deep connections. It's on the leader to model this, so if you're in a leadership position, don't be afraid to admit mistakes or when you don't know an answer.

Challenges You Will Encounter

* Being vulnerable is difficult—it's not natural for many of us to openly admit our flaws and mistakes or when we need help. But with practice, you can learn to be more comfortable with vulnerability.

* Many companies operate by a strictly "all business, no personal" policy. Employees who have spent time in these kinds of organizations will have to be taught to take the time to slow down and connect with their coworkers versus diving right into the business at hand.

7

Impactful In-Person Meetings, Unforgettable Memories, and Deep Bonds

Every year for our holiday party, we take all of our employees and their spouses or guests to a fun destination for a long weekend. One year, we chose New Orleans. It had been seven years since Hurricane Katrina, but the city had not yet recovered. Many people were still displaced from their homes, and the infrastructure needed massive repairs. We decided to cover an extra day in New Orleans for anyone willing to help complete a service project to rehab a children's

community center that had spent a month underwater.

The center's coordinators were accustomed to
working with teams of 15 to 20 people, so when
they saw 250 volunteers jump out of five buses, it was clear that chaos could easily ruin our
intended contribution. It was total disorganiza-
tion at first, but amazingly, within less than an
hour, every single person found a meaningful
activity to jump into—whether it was cleaning debris from the parking lot, painting walls,
building bleachers, or cleaning the mud that
covered everything that had been submerged
underwater. The work was physically demanding and dirty, yet also peaceful and fulfilling.

The conversations, collaboration, and camara-
derie that we experienced were just as important as the significant facelift we gave the community center. By the end of the day, everyone's
energy was completely drained, but our hearts
were filled with a sense of accomplishment
from our work and deepened connections with
one another.

As the buses approached the hotel, we saw a
long line of people standing outside. We were
disappointed, thinking it was one more delay
standing between us and hot showers. But as
we stepped out of the buses, deafening applause

erupted from the hotel staff who lined the entire sidewalk all the way through the hotel lobby. The applause continued as we walked into the hotel, leaving all of us speechless, many of us in tears at what was an emotional climax to a special day and bonding experience. My eyes still tear up every single time I recall the memory.

—Jeff L., Cincinnati, Ohio

Face-to-face meetings cement relationships, energize your teams, and reinforce your culture. Whether your company is completely or partially virtual, geographically close or spread out around the globe, consciously designing in-person interactions is essential to taking your culture from good to great.

Immeasurable ROI

I was taking a speaking class from the instructor who trained Princess Diana in public speaking. I was nervous and intimidated, but he was a master of interpersonal interaction and quickly put me at ease.

One lesson was on the literal energy that ebbs and flows between people as they interact. To demonstrate to us nonbelievers, he produced what looked like a big glass tube capsule containing a lighting system, the ends encircled

with silver.[1] He instructed one person to grab
one end of the capsule, and we all joined hands
in a circle. When the final person closed the circle, grabbing the capsule's open end, an electric
circuit was completed, illuminating the light! If
anyone let go of their neighbor's hand, the circle was broken, and the light went out.

—Larry E., Columbus, Ohio

When we get the entire company together for a
meeting, there is palpable energy in the room. Everyone is energized. Everyone comes away from the
meeting amped up and on a high, excited to work for
Centric and reconnected with our larger purpose—a
feeling that's difficult to replicate virtually. The best
part is seeing people connect in person who so far have
only known each other through email, chat, or phone
calls. We know this because people tell us.

Although impossible to quantify in hard ROI dol-
lars, we know the value of these in-person meetings is
real. Research backs this up: according to an APCO
Insight and MMB survey, 95 percent of small business
owners say meetings produce a positive ROI.[2] The benefits include:

Building new networks. Those serendipitous encounters where you meet someone new who is helpful
to your job simply don't often happen in a virtual environment. Yet new relationships are crucial for fostering collaboration and ideation. In *Creativity, Inc.*, Pixar
founder Edwin Catmull talks about how valuable im-

promptu encounters are to creativity, so much so that Pixar designed its buildings to make sure this happens on a regular basis.[3]

Providing shared experience. Shared experiences help team members know one another better, fostering easier collaboration and higher productivity.[4] This is a tactic used in the military to form strong teams with unbreakable bonds. In *Team of Teams*, General Stanley McChrystal details how the US Navy relies on shared experiences to bond Navy SEALs.[5] Throughout one of their training courses, prospective SEALs are divided up into small teams and required to do literally everything together. Needless to say, they quickly bond into a cohesive team unit.

Fulfilling the psychological need for connection. In the book *Social*, social psychologist and neuroscientist Matthew Lieberman explains that humans need connection just as much as we need food and water.[6] Employees who work from home and don't physically see their coworkers can sometimes feel isolated. Getting together in person provides an extra touchpoint and helps employees feel like a part of something bigger.

There's no way around the fact that getting virtual workers together—especially if they're geographically spread out—can be expensive. We have employees who live in almost every state in the US, and we have a large office in Delhi, India. Our all-company, in-person meetings are a huge expense, amounting to about 6 percent of our net profit.

We look at the line item every year, and every year it's a no-brainer to continue making the investment. We believe all those intangible benefits of getting together are critical to maintaining a great culture as a virtual company. It helps that we save a lot of money on office expenses. We also put a lot of thought into our in-person interactions to maximize the value for the cost.

That said, there are many ways to get together in person, and there's sure to be a fit for your business model, budget, approach to remote work, and culture goals. By experimenting with different in-person interactions, you'll quickly get a feel for what's working and how to optimize the experience (more on that later).

Regardless of whether your company is fully remote or consists of a mix of virtual and in-office workers, you'll want to occasionally get people together in person for all the reasons we listed above, both in large group gatherings consisting of the entire company or smaller subsets of your team, such as different regions, business units, or operating groups.

All Hands on Deck

Companywide and other large gatherings are costly simply because of their size, so you'll likely only be able to afford this a few times each year. We get all of our employees in the US together three times each year, and our employees in India together once. Because these gatherings are infrequent and expensive, we make a huge production out of each one to maximize the benefit and impact. This is what our yearly gatherings look like.

Spring meeting

Our multiday, business-focused spring meeting takes place in one of the US cities where we have operations. We review performance from the last year, lay out our strategy for the year ahead, and offer breakout sessions to expose employees to new offerings and skills. We also have a lot of fun and treat employees to nationally known speakers, live music by the Centric band, games, and surprises. It always feels more like a reunion of old friends than a stodgy business meeting.

Summer meeting

Our summer meeting is another multiday event that takes place at a fun venue in the US. During the first day, we hold a TED Talk- and Hackathon-style event where all of our technologists share the latest tech innovations. Day two is a half day of progress updates on the year's plan, sometimes followed by a community service project, such as building bikes for kids who can't afford them or packaging meals for the homeless.

Winter/holiday party

The story that opened this chapter is from one of Centric's holiday parties. We started this tradition early on because we wanted to break the mold of a traditional, boring, corporate holiday party and treat everyone and their significant others to a weekend trip to celebrate. (We can't afford to fly everyone from India to the US, so we developed the same concept for our India team.)

Our holiday party has no agenda other than to have fun, make great memories, and build better relationships. We've gone to New Orleans, Puerto Vallarta, Cancun, Las Vegas, the Bahamas, San Diego, and many other fun destinations. It is hugely expensive. It is as fun as it sounds. And it's worth every penny. The legendary stories, memories, and friendships that occur are invaluable to building and maintaining our culture. Because we believe culture is the core of our success, we continue to invest in these trips.

Smaller Gatherings

We were traveling to Boston for our annual leadership retreat that occurs every December. The Boston team had mentioned they were working with a tight budget but had been able to find a resort on a lake.

When we pulled in, we were surprised to find our "resort" was actually a kid's summer camp built in the 1930s. Our sleeping accommodations were Quonset hut-style barracks. The one-story buildings had one large, open room with single beds and mattresses—also from the 1930s—lined up dormitory style.

Although there were 14 beds in the large room, I had only two roommates. Before we turned in, I asked if either one snored. Just to be safe, I strategically picked a bed in the corner.

As I tossed and turned with my summer blanket trying to get a little sleep, I heard footsteps. I figured one of my roommates was going to the bathroom. Except the footsteps continued as the person paced back and forth. I curled up, figuring the pacing would stop. It did, but then to my surprise, I felt my bed moving. Opening one eye, I saw my roommate Sam sitting on my bed near my head. He was mumbling about needing to use the bathroom. I pretended to be asleep. Probably not very smart. Thankfully, Sam stood up, found the restroom, then returned to bed.

The next morning, after we talked about the need for full disclosure, Sam said he had a dream he was in a big house and he couldn't find the way out. He said he knew I was in the house and figured I could help him out.

Perhaps it's a coincidence, but the Boston business unit has never hosted another leadership retreat.

—Ted G., Chicago, Illinois

In an all-virtual model, it may not be feasible or affordable to get everyone together. Designing and budgeting for smaller meetings of organizational groups, such as your leadership team or different business units, is a good solution that ensures valuable face-to-face time still occurs regularly.

Your organization likely has numerous groups that would make sense to get together in person. An easy way to break it up is by operating groups, profit-and-loss centers, or cost centers. We've also found it helpful to schedule regular in-person meetings for:

- Groups that frequently add new members and so are lacking in strong relationships

- Groups or business units that require a high degree of collaboration

- Groups or areas with recurring conflict

In addition to Centric's all-company meetings, we empower each of our operating groups to decide when and how often they meet in person. They build this into their budget and plan for the year.

As the story heading up this section noted, we also bring the leadership team together each December; this event is critical for leaders to form relationships with one another. Hard conversations and decisions are part of the job, and if you have met face-to-face and have that interaction as a base, you will be much more prepared to have a hard, yet productive, conversation with another member of the leadership team.

We've occasionally gone a little too far with the frugal accommodations; unfortunately, the summer camp in winter isn't even the worst place we've stayed. I've tried to convince everyone without much success that overcoming our adverse accommodations helps us bond.

Optimizing Your Time Together

> At our face-to-face meeting in the Smoky Mountains, we went ziplining as a team-building exercise. I don't remember the exact name, but it was something like Bubba's Discount Ziplining. We got into our gear and climbed the high tower to start our adventure. The views over the fall mountains were stunning. As we looked a little closer at the mesmerizing view, it sure looked like the branches were close enough to the line that we would hit them as we zipped past. We asked Bubba about our concern. He said "Yep, when you hit 'em, that's when we know we got to trim 'em."
>
> —Jason P., Columbus, Ohio

In an era where only a third of employees are engaged at work, in-person meetings offer an invaluable opportunity to build your culture and get employees excited about your company and proud to be a part of it.[7] The fastest way to get there is by helping your employees make deep connections with their teammates.

When designing an in-person meeting agenda, you should schedule a mix of business and relationship-building activities. The goal is to offer a shared experience that everyone will bond over and talk about for years to come. We design many of our meetings to allow employees to use all of their senses and generate feelings and memories that you would never get from a virtual setting. Some of the activities we've relied on to help build culture include:

Challenging adventures that get you out of your comfort zone

We've gone ATVing, rock climbing, and deep-sea fishing. We've raced (and walked) 5Ks and broken out of escape rooms. There are endless options. Research suggests that voluntarily participating in high arousal negative experiences with other people fosters trust—this is why people love watching scary movies together or riding roller coasters.[8] You don't have to do a sketchy ziplining outfit, but you do want to pick something everyone can participate in and everyone's going to have a little anxiety about.

Local community service

We often try to build service projects into our meetings. The best is when we get to meet with the beneficiaries of the project. We've rehabbed houses, designed software for food banks, and organized coat drives for disadvantaged kids. Afterward, we feel great knowing we've made a difference.

Activities that build business interaction skills

We've done group improv, happiness training, customer service training, and more. Ideally, you want to break groups up to compete against one another and reward the winning team, whether it's with a dollar store medal or simple bragging rights.

Activities that involve employees' families

Once or twice a year, we get together all our families for a fun activity. Why? Because when we hire someone, we want to include their entire family. We've done everything from an annual pumpkin patch visit to family volunteer activities and visits to local museums.

The bottom line is that in-person meetings shouldn't be just about business. Yes, it's important to get work done, but sometimes you need to get together to simply build relationships and reinforce your culture. Teams that play and have fun together outperform teams that are all business all the time—research shows employees who are happier are up to 20 percent more productive.[9]

The important thing is to prioritize these in-person interactions, experiment with which ones create the most value, and budget for these each year.

Finding the Right Mix

Most typical office environments keep people from working efficiently and producing their best work. With so many distractions—like social media and cell phones, not to mention general office interruptions—it's hard to ensure teams are working optimally. For one client, for example, we found that one of their project teams was only working hands-to-keyboard three days a week.

For this client, we decided to test a theory based on the book *Deep Work* by Cal Newport. The theory was: if we take the team and we remove all those distractions, put them in a box, and let them work in a way that makes them focused and more productive, then would that team be more efficient, proficient, and happier?

We took that client's team to our Columbus Development Studio, which we purposefully created with input from build teams to ensure productivity while minimizing distractions. And what we found was that just by changing the environment and creating some rules around interactions, the company (and the team) saw a threefold increase in net productivity.

—Shawn W., Columbus, Ohio

As even the most conservative companies are now allowing employees to work remotely, leaders are having to learn to manage a mixed team, with some employees coming into the office every day while others are partially or permanently remote.

We've done a lot of experimenting to find the right mix of in-person interactions that helps us get our work done, supports healthy team dynamics, and builds culture. While there is no single right answer, the following questions can help you find the best mix for your company:

- How well does the team know each other? How long have they worked together? How well do they collaborate? Teams with a long history together require fewer in-person meetings, if any at all.

- How often do new members join the team? Is there a mix of experienced and new team members? We've found it can be difficult for new team members to join really established teams, but in-person meetings go a long way toward helping them become integrated.

- How well does the team function? Are there trust or cooperation issues? If there are any recurring problems, you'll want to increase in-person meetings and have the difficult conversations until the issue is resolved.

- How seasoned are your new employees? We increasingly hire employees just out of college and have found it's best to train in person when someone is new to the working world—they need more structure and hands-on learning than can be provided virtually.

When determining how often to meet in person, you'll also need to consider customer or client needs. Some clients will need more facetime than others. It's always a good idea to have in-person meetings any time key decisions are being made and you can't afford ambiguity. Big project milestones (project kickoffs, design sessions, celebrations) are also ideally experienced in person to create a better sense of shared responsibility and to move the project forward during critical junctures.

Ultimately, it's up to individual project teams to find balance between in-person and remote work. It's easy to err on the side of too much personal interaction, with pointless status or committee meetings, not to mention interruptions from colleagues and constant notifications from our devices. In the average office environment, where you're interrupted about every three minutes, focus can become elusive.[10]

To remain effective, teams may need to lay some ground rules for getting deep thinking work done, whether they're working from home, at an office, or at a client site. Maybe everyone agrees to put their phones on silent during certain periods of the day. One of my favorite examples is the headphone rule, where everyone on the team has agreed that wearing headphones is equivalent to having a closed office door. Everyone respects the headphones, and everyone can get done what they need to throughout the day.

We also make it a point to build in regular touch-points and interactions with team members whose work requires very little interaction with other employees or clients. Otherwise, these employees can easily feel disconnected and become more likely to quit.[11] According to a Workplace by Facebook survey, 54 percent of remote workers feel voiceless in their organizations.[12] We want to make sure that's never the case with any of our employees.

No Office, No Problem

Even the most difficult parts of running a business can be done without an office. Years ago, we had decided to let an employee go. A conversation this serious always needs to be done face-to-face. I had routinely been meeting this person at a Panera, so I planned for us to meet there at an off-hours time. All kinds of thoughts were running through my head: Will he make a big scene? Is this legal? Will I receive a lifetime ban from Panera with my face on a flyer passed out at every location?

I arrived early and picked a spot away from everyone in the store. Just as the employee sat down, an older gentleman skipped all of the empty tables and sat right next to us. I was thinking "Dude, you are killing me." I decided to go ahead and have the discussion anyway. It ended up being very cordial. While the older gentleman never looked at us, I'm fairly sure he listened to every word.

—Larry E., Columbus, Ohio

I regularly get asked how we operate without a normal office environment. Centric has operations in 12 US cities, and in most of these, we operate without office space. In some cases, however, we do temporarily use shared office space or development studios (physical office space where we spin project teams up and down). Because our business is consulting, our employees are not only working from home or at one of these office sites, but they're also regularly working at client sites.

With so many employees running all over the place, our in-person meetings are vital to making sure everyone feels connected and part of the team. In addition to the spaces listed above, "free space" can be an easy way to get together. By free space, I mean any nontraditional venue you meet to conduct business, such as a coffee shop, hotel lobby, or restaurant (usually you have to buy a drink or food to use the space). Centric uses free space for many different functions, including:

- Sub-team meetings: For example, our business development team meets once a week at a restaurant with a private room.

- Business unit meetings: We hold quarterly meetings with every employee in a business unit or city. The location varies but always involves a private room to conduct the meeting. We usually follow the business portion of the gathering with a fun social activity.

- Project team meetings: A few times each month, project teams get together for lunch or after-work drinks to build their team dynamic.

- Individual coaching and mentoring sessions: A few times a year, individual employees and their mentors meet in person over breakfast or lunch.

You'd be amazed at how many options for free space are out there. In one of the cities where we do business, the Dunkin' Donuts has the nicest private boardroom in town.

In other words, don't be afraid to use free space for real business discussions—we've had everything from salary negotiations to performance reviews (even difficult ones) in free space. So much so that we've often joked that we should buy stock in Panera. We leverage their community rooms for a lot of meetings, and most of our recruiting meetings are at Starbucks or a restaurant.

Clients also don't mind meeting in free space. We've rarely had anyone request to meet at our office. When they do, we explain we've kept our rates lower by keeping our internal cost down. We've never had an issue.

An important caveat: you do need to match the business function with the type of venue you choose. A business development meeting where you're going to share important confidential information requires a private space. An interview or performance review can be conducted at someone's favorite restaurant—unless it's a bad review. The last thing you want is to forever ruin someone's favorite restaurant.

Free space can also be a great option for culture-building activities—think wine tasting, go-kart racing, laser tag, or ice cream making (all hits at Centric). Again, the key to culture is how you go about building relationships. It's about the quality and type of conversations you have, not where you meet. The reason an employee stays with you is about the people relationships, their career growth, and the type of work they are doing. Having a hip office is usually way down on the priority list, especially when those higher-priority needs are exceeded.[13]

The main point here is that if your virtual company or team is in close geographic proximity, make it a point to meet up. It's easy to get lazy about getting together—everyone's busy. While these in-person touchpoints take time and effort, they're invaluable in sustaining culture and building all-star teams.

Quick Read Summary

- In-person meetings are a powerful way to take your virtual culture to a new level.

- In-person meetings can be expensive but have a huge ROI: they help employees deepen relationships founded virtually, develop new networks, and feel excited and engaged about their work.

- To get the most out of your in-person meetings, you have to consider the type and frequency of these interactions. We found it's best to combine business and team building, relationship building, or fun.

- If you don't have office space, free space (coffee shops, restaurants, etc.) provide a lot of options and can be an effective way to get work done.

- The key to culture is how you build relationships. It's about the quality and types of conversations you have, not where you have them.

How to Get Started Designing In-Person Meetings

- Think through how often in-person meetings need to occur and whether you need to get the entire company together, segment it up by smaller groups, or a mix.

- To get the most bang for your buck, make sure to build in time for activities that strengthen culture, whether by deepening relationships, getting people out of their comfort zone, or participating in a charitable activity.

- Don't forget this is a major investment: large meetings especially are going to cost you, but the ROI is well worth the money and effort.

- Consider free spaces that exist where you operate and how you can use them to help people connect in person both to get work done and reinforce culture.

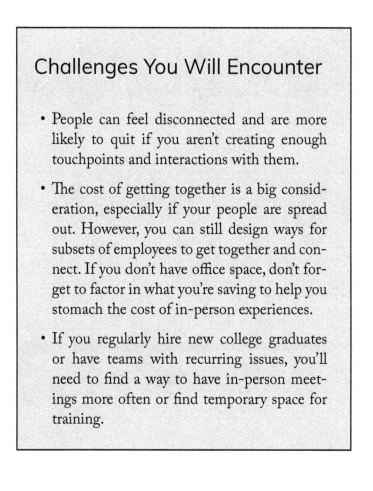

Challenges You Will Encounter

• People can feel disconnected and are more likely to quit if you aren't creating enough touchpoints and interactions with them.

• The cost of getting together is a big consideration, especially if your people are spread out. However, you can still design ways for subsets of employees to get together and connect. If you don't have office space, don't forget to factor in what you're saving to help you stomach the cost of in-person experiences.

• If you regularly hire new college graduates or have teams with recurring issues, you'll need to find a way to have in-person meetings more often or find temporary space for training.

8

Continuous Feedback, Continuous Culture Improvement

Like every company, we expected an occasional disgruntled employee. What we didn't expect was that disgruntled employees would share their (often misleading) gripes for the world to see. When we discovered our negative reviews on Glassdoor, our first reaction was just to ignore them. Maybe no one else would notice?

We quickly learned this strategy wouldn't work—candidates were seeing the reviews and coming to inaccurate conclusions about Centric. The reviews were damaging our hard-earned reputation and negatively influencing our recruiting pipeline.

So we went to the other extreme. We embraced Glassdoor. We began responding to each and every review, even the nasty, negative ones. We asked our current employees to leave their honest feedback. We even encouraged candidates to check us out on the site.

The results shocked us: visits to our Glassdoor employer profile increased 700 percent, our Glassdoor rating improved from 3.5 to 4.5 in six months, and Glassdoor became a top source of traffic to our corporate website. We even won the Glassdoor 2016 Best Places to Work and Top CEO awards, which resulted in multiple media pickups and numerous social media mentions.

Most importantly, we got honest feedback, both good and bad, from current and past employees. We learned new things about our company culture. And we had the opportunity to share our story authentically.

—Carmen F., Cleveland, Ohio

Great culture can't exist without feedback—otherwise, you get off track, parts of your culture get lost during growth periods or grow stale over time, and employees feel unheard. This applies to every business, virtual or not. But for entirely virtual companies, regular feedback is especially critical. With limited in-person interactions, you have to take extra, deliberate steps to get feedback and understand how employees are feeling. You can't rely on those impromptu encounters in the office to discover an issue is brewing.

Think about how often feedback pops up in your life outside of work. We're used to rating every imaginable product and service online, voicing both the good and the bad, and contributing to a vast data pool that helps companies improve. Why should the workplace be any different?

Research has a lot to say about the value of soliciting employee feedback:

- A 2017 workplace study found a positive correlation between employee engagement and giving employees an outlet to voice their feedback, frustrations, and motivations.[1]

- The Society for Human Resource Management says constant employee feedback is key to building a culture of engaged employees.[2]

- A Gallup poll found companies that give employees regular opportunities for feedback have 14.9 percent lower turnover rates than companies with no feedback mechanisms.[3]

It makes sense: when you ask employees for feedback, it signals that their opinions, experiences, and ideas matter.

But it's not enough to collect feedback. You have to act on it and show employees you're listening to their concerns and ideas. Research from as far back as the 1920s illustrates why this matters.[4] Researchers at a Western Electric manufacturing plant found employee productivity increased any time any change was made to the workplace, such as turning the lights up or down. In discussing the results with the workers, the researchers found that workers felt more valued because they felt like someone was paying attention to them. In other words, when your employees feel heard, they also feel motivated. This is known as the Hawthorne Effect, and while the study's results have been called into question over the years, the main takeaway rings true: your employees need to know you care. Acting on their feedback is an effective way to demonstrate this.

We've built multiple methods to get and give feedback at both companywide and individual levels. We use these processes to improve our culture, keep a pulse on how employees are feeling, address individual employee concerns, and guide employee development. Some of the most meaningful, impactful changes we've made as a company have come from feedback, and feedback has been fundamental to the preservation and growth of our culture over the years.

Company-Level Feedback

Part of my job is making Centric's vision for a great culture and unmatched experiences a reality. Every year, I use our employee satisfaction survey to identify and address the top employee concerns. Years ago, our three-week paid time off policy was routinely mentioned but never a top priority. But after addressing some of the higher-priority areas, our PTO policy rocketed to the top of the list with over 75 percent of our employees indicating it was a concern. Immediate action was needed!

As we redesigned our PTO policy, we had two goals: to provide our employees with an unmatched experience without generating a lot of new expense and to ensure minimal administrative overhead. I researched what competitors and clients were doing and found an endless array of options but none that fit our needs. We eventually landed on a self-managed PTO policy, a unique approach that aligned with our culture. Under this policy, we don't limit the amount of PTO, but we do provide a set of guardrails for people to consider as they plan their days off. We want it to be clear that we expect people to take the PTO they need while respecting the system.

It's been over 10 years since we implemented our self-managed PTO policy. We've analyzed the results multiple times over the years and walked away each time knowing the change we made was the right one. I've spoken with many

people from other companies who are amazed
the policy worked and has scaled. To me, that
was never a concern. I knew if we kept hiring
people who fit with our culture and treated
them well, there's no reason to think the PTO
policy would be abused.

—Matt H., Hartford, Connecticut

Companywide feedback allows us to gauge overall
employee satisfaction, pinpoint any cultural issues, and
prioritize where we should focus our time.

We've experimented with a number of different
tools and processes, everything from artificial intel-
ligence tools that identify at-risk employees to mi-
cro-pulse surveys that give daily immediate feedback.
We've found the most effective tools incorporate the
following components.

Anonymous feedback

You should engage at least one tool that allows for
anonymous feedback, because the only way you can
truly uncover and address issues is to get the full, un-
varnished truth of how people are feeling. Even when
you encourage a culture of transparency and make it
okay to give feedback without fear, human nature is
hard to overcome. Anonymity helps employees feel
they can voice concerns honestly without putting their
job or relationship with their team or manager on the
line.

Josh Bersin, founder of Bersin by Deloitte, an HR research firm, captures the importance of anonymity: "In the consumer world, if you poorly review a restaurant or down rate a driver, there are likely no major consequences to you—in fact it can be a good thing, because the company can get back to you to address your problem. At work, the ramifications are different. If you down rate your boss or say something critical about him (even in a constructive way), you may be labeled a troublemaker, which now reflects poorly on you."[5]

Knowing this, Centric's internal company satisfaction survey is anonymous. External public feedback sites like Glassdoor are also anonymous and worth keeping an eye on for valuable insights. Yes, you will get the occasional unfair, untrue post. But overall, sites like Glassdoor help you pinpoint your consistent wins and misses. If you are truly living your core values and building the culture you want, you shouldn't fear being completely open for the world to see. Plus, in the age of social media, openness and transparency are a given—you don't have much of a choice in the matter.

Quantifiable data

Management expert Peter Drucker famously said, "If you can't measure it, you can't improve it." This is true for feedback and—by extension—culture. Feedback is only actionable if you can spot patterns and trends. For that, you need quantifiable data. Many companies are turning to people analytics, one of the fastest growing areas of HR, to mine employee data to understand how people work and how they can improve employee experiences and performance.[6]

We use a widely accepted method called Net Promotor Score (NPS) to measure employee and client satisfaction.[7] There's a lot of science behind NPS, but the short version is that it's a simple way of scoring your customers' and employees' satisfaction and loyalty levels. You ask them a question along the lines of "On a scale of 1 to 10, how likely are you to recommend Centric to a friend?" You then calculate your NPS by subtracting the percentage of those who wouldn't recommend you from the percentage of those who would.

For employees, we design additional survey questions that help us determine how well we're living our culture. These include:

- "I believe the leaders of this organization are honest and trustworthy." (Are we living our core value of integrity?)

- "There is open and forthright communication between employees and leadership." (Are we modeling a culture of transparency?)

- "What should we start doing?" (What is something new that would enhance our culture?)

We conduct these surveys once a year, and they're always anonymous. Because NPS is widely used, we can easily benchmark how well we're doing for our industry. While the tool isn't perfect (what is?), it does allow us to measure the health of our culture and shows us which areas need improvement.

Once we started using quantifiable measures, we began reaping countless insights from the data. We started to see trends, such as which business groups score low and where we might have some cultural issues.

Rapid two-way feedback

A little over half of companies perform annual employee engagement surveys.[8] But they're increasingly turning to other less formal forms of employee feedback, and for good reason: formal surveys provide just yearly datapoints, leaving plenty of time for new issues to crop up and balloon out of control.[9] Not to mention that companies make many major decisions throughout the year that impact employees and culture. When an issue or policy decision of any magnitude comes up, you'll want to first get rapid feedback from a cross-section of employees and engage with them directly to dig deeper into their insights.

There are countless apps these days that allow companies to collect rapid feedback. Niko Niko, for example, is a Japanese app that lets employees share their mood with a simple emoji (smiley, flat, frown), giving managers an instant peek into how employees are feeling and alerting them immediately of any issues.[10]

We rely on our Voice of the Employee (VOTE) Advisory Team. Made up of a rotating selection of employees from all levels and backgrounds, VOTE provides transparent, immediate feedback on any potential major decisions, especially those impacting culture. The team gives us an idea of how an issue will be viewed by the company as a whole and an arena for iterating different approaches before we roll something out to the entire business.

External feedback

While most of your mechanisms for gathering cultural feedback will be internal, you also want to collect feedback from customers, partners, and employees who have recently left the company. As outsiders (or nearly outsiders), they can give you a fresh perspective on how well you're living up to your values.

There are three sources of external feedback Centric monitors, two of which we've already discussed: client satisfaction via NPS, Glassdoor reviews, and in-depth exit interviews. Employees who are on their way out tend to be open about anything that wasn't great, and we often uncover an opportunity for improvement. The interview questions are designed to help us rate our culture and see where we can do better. For example:

- "What three things could your manager and/or Centric leadership do to improve?"

- "Was there anything we haven't discussed that could have been done to positively affect your experience at Centric?"

- "For a qualified friend or colleague, how likely are you to recommend Centric as a good place to work?"

Once you have feedback, what do you do with it? Here is where the hard work begins. You'll need to figure out if you really do have issues that need to be addressed, determine their root causes, and decide which ones need to be prioritized.

Our talent management group first analyzes the data to identify recurring issues or potential problem areas. We then spin up a mini team or assign one of our leaders to determine whether we need to dig deeper. Once we've researched an issue and determined we need to take action, we add it to our list of projects or assign it to a leader to address. Common examples include:

Declining satisfaction scores. Occasionally, one of our operating groups will see a sudden drop in overall satisfaction or for a particular area. When that happens, we talk to employees within that group to get more context, identify a root cause, and create an action plan. In one case, we were able to identify that a newly promoted leader needed additional training on how to better interact with employees. The declining scores tipped us off about the problem, but it wasn't until we interviewed a subset of employees that we pinpointed the issue.

Recurring issues. Often, an area that needs improvement will repeatedly show up on exit interviews and our employee satisfaction survey. Vacation policy, career training, and onboarding are just a few examples of issues causing major heartburn that we've tackled over the years. When we identify a problem area, we assign a project team to research the issue, develop alternatives, and engineer a solution.

Culture-enhancing ideas. Purposeful, frequent feedback not only helps us determine what's not working, but it's also a wonderful source of new ideas to enhance our culture. A few examples of ideas that have been suggested by our employees include sending annual Mother's Day gifts to all employee and spouse moms, conducting an annual one-day tech innovation summit for our technologists, and producing Ask Me Anything videos featuring our top leaders.

Individual-Level Feedback

> For six years, I strenuously worked to build a successful technology practice within Centric. My modus operandi was to drive teams hard and get things done. However, I was blind to the reality that I was difficult to work with. My team felt unappreciated, and my relationships with them felt transactional. Eventually the practice hit a wall; I could no longer use brute force for every client project. Growth stagnated, and people on my team left the company in a state of dissatisfaction.
>
> In any other organization, I would have been shown the door, and I expect this option was

seriously considered. Miraculously, my bosses gave me another option: work with an outside coach to develop an awareness of how my actions affect other people and learn how to help others on my team do the same. This was the hardest thing I ever attempted in my career, yet it saved my job and dramatically enriched my personal life. The technology practice has since achieved new heights: our team size is exploding, and I'm happier in my career than ever before.

It takes a true leader to recognize human potential through the fog of poor performance. While most people are naturally adept at basic human interactions, there are people who deeply desire strong relationships yet struggle mightily to make the necessary behavioral changes. I was firmly in the latter group. Centric's culture and leaders have been a blessing to me, and I remain deeply appreciative (and also amazed) that they gave me the chance to correct my course.

—Jeff K., Columbus, Ohio

When you're virtual, it's critical that leaders maintain close, personal connections with their team members. When you don't see someone walking around the office, it's easy to forget to do even a quick check-in. Here's how we keep this top of mind at Centric.

Regular temperature checks

An old leadership saying, "You can't coach from the press box," speaks to the need to get out of your office if you want to keep a pulse on what's going on. The virtual equivalent is that you can't ignore your company's virtual chat rooms. You should be constantly reaching out and checking in on people.

Again, virtual employees can quickly feel disconnected from the company without regular interactions. Lacking the visual cues of the office environment, a problem can fester before you ever hear about it. You want to catch any feelings of disconnection before employees start looking for a new job—this can only be done if you're regularly reaching out to your direct reports and "checking their temperature."

And business-related conference calls won't cut it. You need to allocate one-on-one time (in person or virtual) to check in with individual employees to connect on a personal level and give them an opportunity to share any worries. By building in this one-on-one time—which, by the way, shouldn't feel like a sacrifice, given that in-office employees spend about 8 percent of their time socializing—employees will feel more comfortable bringing up issues when they arise.[11] Without an established, trusted relationship, they'll feel awkward starting those difficult conversations and might even leave before you realize there's a problem.

No such thing as too much feedback

The one thing we hear continuously from our employees is how much they crave performance feedback. Especially millennials,[12] who will make up 75 percent of the workforce by 2025.[13]

But it's not just feedback per se that employees crave—they also want coaching as they develop their careers.[14] Research shows employees value culture and career growth much more than compensation and benefits.[15] Giving them what they want is a win-win. Employees get help climbing the career ladder, and you get more skilled, more engaged workers who are more likely to stick around.[16]

We've developed an elaborate individual feedback and development process. We assign each employee a feedback manager, who collects all feedback and development ideas for the individual and provides the comments at agreed-upon intervals. Every employee can choose to work with a coach if they feel they need help. About 20 percent of our employees take this route. They meet with their coach regularly as they develop a career-development plan, and the coach holds them accountable. Finally, each employee can also choose to have one or more informal mentors who provide career advice as needed.

As Jeff's story above illustrates, when employees feel their company is investing a lot in their growth, they feel part of something bigger. They develop loyalty to the company, knowing there's a two-way street for communicating issues and ideas and getting the support they need to succeed.

Quick Read Summary

- You can (and should!) measure your company culture. Using tools like Net Promoter Score surveys and including questions around your core values and culture allow you to see where you are doing well and what you need to work on. Additional tools such as exit interviews and Glassdoor provide an authentic picture of how well you are doing on culture and how employees are feeling.

- Asking for employee feedback just once a year via the traditional employee survey isn't enough—you need to build in regular touchpoints with employees on a companywide and individual level to keep a pulse on your culture and employee satisfaction.

- Maintaining and growing culture is hard, never-ending work. The feedback from these tools and processes has allowed us to maintain and grow a healthy culture for over 20 years.

How to Get Started Creating a Culture of Continuous Feedback

- Determine how often you want feedback and how you're going to get it. Centric uses a mixture of anonymous companywide surveys, exit interviews, external feedback via sites like Glassdoor, and touchpoints with individual employees.

- Make sure you build in some form of feedback that's quantifiable, such as Net Promoter Score, so you can track your progress and identify trends and problem areas.

- Consider how you'll get rapid employee feedback when you're considering any big changes throughout the year that will affect culture.

Challenges You Will Encounter

- People won't always be willing to give you frequent and candid feedback. That said, a lot of tools are available that make the process

less painful, such as pulse surveys. We continue to leverage the latest technology to get
as much data as we can about the health of
our culture.

9

Crappy Collaboration Tools Can Sink Your Culture

I was touring the new office of the CEO of a fast-growing company. They had spared no expense, and the space was beautiful—exposed brick and wood beams, a gourmet kitchen, the latest high-end furniture. While describing the state-of-the-art phone and video system they had installed, the CEO mentioned he was still getting over the sticker shock. He asked, "What do you guys do for your phone system?" I replied, "www.freeconferencecall.com." He slowly shook his head, not saying a word.

—Larry E., Columbus, Ohio

In the early days of Centric, I was proud of our frugal mindset. We kept our overhead low by avoiding many of the costs of having office space and spending as little as possible on our technology infrastructure. We relied on tools that barely got the job done—basic email and conference call platforms, low-end document sharing and collaboration capabilities, low-feature accounting software. The list goes on and on.

What I've since come to realize is that skimping on software that helps you virtually connect and collaborate ends up hurting your company. Before we started properly investing in tech tools, we were highly inefficient in all of our internal processes. Everything took more time and manpower than it should have. Our employees were frustrated. They spent every day fighting technology to get work done.

Our virtual culture suffered because our remote employees weren't able to effectively connect and collaborate. We knew something had to change.

We vetted our options and ultimately selected Microsoft Teams for its ability to offer communication and collaboration tools on a single platform. Yes, it was considerably more expensive than our free conference call service. But the investment was money well spent (and long overdue). We felt the positive impact immediately. Our productivity increased, and we became a more connected, cohesive organization.

We immediately saw a 25 percent reduction in email traffic. Instead of flooding everyone's inboxes, we were connecting through more effective mediums. We started using video calls, resulting in fewer misunderstandings. We were sharing messages through threaded workstreams, improving transparency. If our communication channels were previously like a pothole-riddled back road, now they are more like a smooth superhighway. Suddenly, collaboration was nearly effortless, and we were completing projects in half the time.

You don't have to take my word for it. A number of independent research firms have shown the significant ROI that the right collaboration products can achieve.[1] Benefits include a reduction in training and onboarding costs, fewer meetings, lower turnover, higher employee satisfaction, and increased productivity.

These days, you really have no excuse for repeating our mistakes. The universe of affordable, cloud-based collaboration tools has exploded in recent years, and suitable options are available for virtual companies of every size. Gartner predicts the market for collaboration tools will reach $4.8 billion by 2023.[2] While you're vetting your options, check out Gartner's "Digital Workplace," which tracks and reports communication tools. The report even includes a sub-category for "Employee Experience Tech," listing tools that relate to employee experience and culture (think workstream collaboration and social connection graphs).

Tools to Build Culture

"We're losing too many recruits; we need to modernize our intranet." I was a bit surprised at this comment from our biotech client, largely because the two phrases didn't seem to connect with each other. It soon became apparent, however, that the public view of the company—the progressive science, community involvement, patient-centric messaging—and the internal experience of the employee were miles apart. Groups of highly talented scientists, operations, and HR team members would accept a position only to leave within six months due in part to this chasm between the public persona of the company and the outdated, stuffy toolset the employees had to work with.

—Aaron A., Hamilton, Ohio

In addition to facilitating great work, the right tools can also make or break your culture. I've heard over and over again how technology creates a barrier in our ability to connect with one another. But I've actually come to believe the exact opposite: technology makes it easier to build culture and real connections. Technology does this by:

Introducing new hires to your culture

When a new employee joins our company, they have access to our collaboration platform, including a historical thread of communications. We encourage them to poke around a bit so they can quickly get a feel for how we do work and how we treat one another. As one new employee recently said: "It is obvious Centric walks the talk by the conversations I see on Microsoft Teams." In short, a good tool will efficiently and effectively demonstrate your culture to new hires.

Allowing you to build virtual communities

> With Veterans Day approaching, I decided to reach out and connect with my fellow veterans at Centric. I had been with the company for a year and had met two other veterans but knew there were more. I could have sent out emails, but I doubt much of a discussion would have transpired, nor would we have been able to easily swap stories or engage in the typical inter-service rivalry and banter.
>
> Instead, I created a virtual team on our collaboration platform and invited all of our veterans to the group. It was the perfect space for us all to interact, coordinate meetups, discuss how to recruit more veterans to Centric, and pass along information about veteran-specific concerns, such as healthcare and insurance.
>
> Almost immediately, we did what every veteran does—talk trash about the other branches (in a mostly friendly manner). Thankfully, trash talking works just as well in a virtual environment as it does face-to-face. We also uploaded

photos to share what we looked like in uniform serving our nation.

Whenever we hire a veteran now, our HR department tells them about our virtual team. When they first join the group, they can see everything we've ever shared. They immediately feel a closer bond to their fellow veterans and engaged as a new employee.

—Mike M., US Army Lieutenant Colonel (retired), Columbus, Ohio

With technology, we can build virtual communities across the company, whether it's a group of employees working on the same project or a group of individuals with something in common (such as our community of veterans). Without the right tools, it would be much harder for virtual employees to connect and build a deeper relationship. With the right tools, our employees have a richer experience and a sense of belonging.

Encouraging transparency

Workplace transparency has been linked with lowered employee stress,[3] increased employee engagement[4] and morale,[5] and other benefits. Transparency also creates a culture of trust.

Modern collaboration tools encourage organizational transparency by creating a searchable, open record of conversations and documents. For example, if I miss a conversation with my team, I can see the historical thread or listen to a recording of the call and be up to speed. Having a complete and accessible record of information also helps employees make better decisions when they're serving clients.

Most tools have built-in security capabilities so you can customize who can access what information. We typically err on the side of transparency, sharing almost all data across the entire company, with the exception of HR data such as salaries and reviews.

Breaking down silos

Effective collaboration tools allow employees to go directly to the source of information they need. These tools essentially flatten your organization, improving the flow of information and making leadership much more accessible.

As a leadership team, we decided we wanted a virtual open door. Anyone can see that I'm available online and chat with me. Gone are the days when an employee looked at an org chart and went through a couple of managers to connect with a higher-up. It works both ways: if I have a question, I can get it answered quickly without having to schedule a meeting. Once our employees became comfortable with our virtual open door, interactions between leadership and employees increased.

In other words, collaboration tools break down organizational silos, helping us get work done efficiently. They allow us to quickly spin up a multidisciplinary team of people from all over the company who work together through a shared virtual space.

Helping build relationships

One leader in our company recently shared how he works with another busy leader. Both of their days are always packed, and if they had to schedule time to get on the phone or play phone tag all day, they would rarely talk. However, with tools that allow them to work on shared documents or text and share workstreams, they interact constantly—seamless communication, no phone calls necessary. This would have been impossible with more rudimentary tools.

Great collaboration tools offer multiple communication channels, creating a melting pot of communication (think chat, video, shared documents, etc.). This allows each person to contribute in a way that feels comfortable.

Even better, these different modes of communication allow employees to share their personality in different ways, whether through sharing content on chat channels, liking posts, or chatting one-on-one or with the team. Everyone gets to know everyone else a little better, which builds trust and leads to strong relationships.

Facilitating collaboration across generations

> A client wanted a strategy for improving collaboration across the organization. The catalyst for the project was twofold: One, they were facing a high number of retirements in the next few years and needed to capture that intellectual property before it was too late. Two, people they were hiring right out of college only stayed with the organization an average of 18 months. In their exit interviews, they cited a lack of modern communication and collaboration tools as a key factor in their decision to leave. Unfortunately, the client ended up rejecting the changes we suggested. When they started announcing layoffs and downsizing, we weren't surprised.
>
> —Joe H., Columbus, Ohio

To retain young, digitally native workers, you have no choice but to provide a modern digital work experience. At the same time, you have to meet the needs and preferences of more experienced workers.

It's a challenge unique to the times—more generations are working together now than ever before.[6] As the diagram on the next page shows, each generation has different preferences for communication.[7] Baby Boomers and Gen X workers like email, while a typical

	Baby Boomer (1946 – 1964)	Generation X (1965 – 1979)	Millennial (1980 – 1997)	Generation Z (1998 – 2020)
In Person Meeting	Always Prefer	Mostly Prefer	Mostly Prefer	Always Prefer
Virtual Online Meeting (No Video)	Mostly Prefer	Always Prefer	Always Prefer	Somewhat Prefer
Virtual Online Meeting (Video)	Do Not Prefer	Occasionally Prefer	Always Prefer	Always Prefer
Outlook Email	Always Prefer	Always Prefer	Somewhat Prefer	Do Not Prefer
Team Workspaces	Always Prefer	Always Prefer	Always Prefer	Always Prefer
Instant Message (IM)	Mostly Prefer	Always Prefer	Always Prefer	Mostly Prefer
Enterprise Social Networking	Do Not Prefer	Occasionally Prefer	Mostly Prefer	Mostly Prefer
Persistent Chat	Do Not Prefer	Occasionally Prefer	Somewhat Prefer	Always Prefer
Conversational User Interfaces	Do Not Prefer	Do Not Prefer	Somewhat Prefer	Always Prefer

Legend:
- ● Always Prefer
- ◕ Mostly Prefer
- ◑ Somewhat Prefer
- ◔ Occasionally Prefer
- ○ Do Not Prefer

Gen Z worker would be happy to never see another email again. Millennials, on the other hand, love team workspaces and instant messaging.

This is another reason why you need tools that support multiple communication channels—you want each worker to have options when it comes to how they get their work done and how they communicate with their team members.

If you shut out sections of your workforce by selecting tools that limit how work can get done, you'll end up with less communication and strained relationships. Some workers won't feel included, which is bad for engagement and can be a serious roadblock to creating a great virtual culture.

Improving work-life balance

Collaboration tools allow anyone to work from anywhere at any time. While some worry that this hyper-connectedness hurts work-life balance, I've seen many employees use these tools to their advantage. The right company policies and guidelines make all the difference.

When an employee can access everything they need from their phone, they're no longer tied to a desk or an office. They have flexibility to get work done when it is best for them. It's no problem to fit in an afternoon school play, a midday yoga practice, or a quick errand.

Modern collaboration tools also allow employees to customize how and when they receive information.

They can set preferences for when they get notifications, which information is provided as a digest, and more. Many tools even have "quiet hours," helping employees unplug outside of work.

Providing data to drive organizational collaboration

Once a collaboration tool is up and running, it can collect data on every imaginable interaction—every email, every chat, every document shared, every meeting attended. This is valuable stuff, as it gives you a detailed look at how collaboration is working in your company and how you can improve. Determining whether you collaborate well requires a mix of art and science, but the data can help you answer questions such as:

- How effective are we at XYZ kind of work?

- Which groups are collaborating the most? Which are collaborating the least?

- Are leaders regularly connecting with one another?

- What does the social graph of the company look like? (How is information flowing?)

- Are the right groups interacting? Is sales interacting with marketing and R&D?

- Are the right people talking to the right people at the right frequency?

Improving the employee experience

It's old news by now that a company's bottom line is tied directly to employee engagement. One study found that companies with high employee engagement could be four times as profitable as companies with average engagement.[8]

Investing in the right tools is critical to ensuring your culture and your employee experience remain positive. We've said it many times throughout this book, but it bears repeating again: culture is cultivated. It is hard to build and easy to lose. The ROI on giving your team the right tools to do their work is immeasurable—but profound.

Quick Read Summary

- Don't skimp on collaboration tools—it's a worthwhile investment with huge ROI that increases collaboration, improves communication, and enhances culture.

- Collaboration tools are available for virtual companies large and small. Gartner's "Digital Workplace" is a useful resource. The report lists communication tools, including a subcategory for culture-related tech.

How to Get Started Using Collaboration Tools

• When vetting your options, remember the right collaboration tool is a serious investment with big ROI potential. It can revolutionize how you work, collaborate, and communicate.

• Think through how collaboration tools can improve your culture. For example, the right tool can help new hires "get" your culture, enable virtual community building, break down silos, and help build relationships.

Challenges You Will Encounter

• Any successful rollout of a tool is one-third technology and two-thirds people. Make sure you have strong governance, guidelines, and change management practices in place with any new tool you introduce.

- Having one isolated department use a great tool will provide little value—you need critical mass, with the entire company using the same technology.

- If you have a bad culture, rolling out a new tool isn't going to fix it. Collaboration tools are an enhancement, not a cure.

10

The Secrets to Becoming an Outstanding Virtual Team Member

Over the past seven years, I've gone through two major transitions: the transition from a 30-year military career to the civilian sector, followed by the transition from working in a traditional office environment to working in a purely virtual environment out of my home.

Each change required significant adjustments on my part, as well as for my entire family. I originally thought that working from home would be an easy, positive transition. Then reality hit—my days were less rigid and less predictable.

My workdays suddenly extended into the evenings on a regular basis. Handling quick "honey dos" and errands became the norm since I was "just sitting on my butt on the couch" (partially kidding here). Plus, the dogs always wanted my attention and always seemed to bark during calls. Unusual background noises were unheard of in my previous brick-and-mortar company (though pretty common in the army).

—Mike M., Columbus, Ohio

Becoming an effective virtual team member who helps build a company's culture is a learned skill, and we've discovered many secrets to success over the years. This chapter is intended to help anyone becoming a remote worker for the first time. I covered some of the material earlier in the book, but I repeat the concepts here in a way that makes it easy for a new remote worker to follow step by step.

The Biggest Challenge for Remote Workers Isn't What You Think It Is

Many new remote workers worry they'll be distracted by their home life and lack the discipline to get work done. Instead, the exact opposite usually occurs: remote workers become more productive once they're freed from a traditional office environment. Perhaps this shouldn't be a surprise, because working remotely means fewer distractions, no commute, and the opportunity to take real breaks. Instead of the dreaded afternoon slump, you can stay fresh and energized all day.

A productivity increase is good, but many remote workers take it too far and end up working too much. According to recent research, remote workers put in more than 40 hours per week 43 percent more frequently than traditional office workers.[1]

How does this happen? The boundaries between your personal and work lives disappear. The laptop is always right there in front of you, and your mobile phone is always on. Your ability to jump between work and personal tasks is suddenly a lot easier, but if you switch back and forth all day long, it quickly adds up. Before you know it, late-night work sessions can become the norm—hardly ideal.

I've found the best approach is to create healthy boundaries around work. Based on your life schedule, determine the time periods during business hours that are strictly for work and when you'll be taking breaks. Develop the discipline to respect those times so you can achieve a healthy balance. And share your approach with your family so they know when to leave you alone so you can stay focused on work.

Being virtual isn't about working more. It's about better work-life balance, which leads to happier, more productive employees who in turn create a great culture.

You've Got the Power

When you begin to work remotely, you'll need to form new habits and make decisions around how you'll get work done. The way your day flows is up to you now (to an extent). You get to architect a customized approach. This requires some experimentation, but here are some of the initial considerations.

Where will you work?

Find a space where you can work free of interruptions and distractions. This could be another bedroom, your basement, a home office, or simply a carved-out area of your apartment. If possible, your workspace should be away from your main living space to reduce the temptation to check in outside of work hours. Make sure your family or roommates understand that when you're in your work area, you shouldn't be bothered. My kids have learned not to interrupt me when my den door is closed (my wife thinks this doesn't apply to her).

When will you work?

Remote workers usually have some flexibility on when they can start and finish work (of course, this has to align with your job's core business day). Establish when you'll be working, and resist the temptation to let work tasks bleed into your personal time. If you're not a morning person, perhaps you start your day later and have a window late in the evening to finish up. If you get your best work done in the morning, maybe you get an early start and end midafternoon.

What kind of break will refresh you?

Take advantage of being remote to do the things you couldn't do if you were stuck at the office. You can exercise midday, run an errand, take your child to lunch, and more. Schedule time to do the things that keep you happy and energized. I've seen over and over again how doing this actually helps you do better work and accomplish more by the end of the day. Research backs this up: according to a 2011 study from the University of Illinois, workers who take regular breaks outperform those who don't.[2]

Where will you go when you need to get out of the house?

Sometimes there will be too many distractions at home, or you just need to get out of the house and interact with people. In the gig economy, many restaurants are completely accustomed to customers working for hours at a table. Coffee shops are a popular choice with remote workers, and for good reason. The ambient noise of a coffee shop is usually around 70 decibels—the optimum level to boost creativity.[3] Find the locations that work best for you and determine how often you'll want a change of scenery.

How will you stay connected with your coworkers?

Working from home can be lonely. Depending on your job requirements, you may have periods where you don't interact with coworkers for a large part of the day. To combat this, schedule regular time to catch up with coworkers. Meet up at a coffee shop or grab lunch. Or, if you have a physical office close by, schedule time to come in once a week.

If you don't live near any coworkers, schedule a virtual lunch where you eat and catch up over video chat. It's also important to connect virtually with coworkers throughout the day, whether through email, chatting over Teams, or giving them a quick call.

How will you remain focused?

New remote workers almost always fall victim to multitasking. It's just too tempting, especially during conference calls ("I'm going to get through these emails during this boring part of the call"). But when you try to do more than one thing at a time, your efficiency nosedives[4] and you're more likely to make mistakes.[5] And when it comes to calls, it's inconsiderate.

To become an accomplished remote worker, you must learn to overcome multitasking temptations and be present for the single task you're working on. If you're on a conference call, focus solely on the conference call (consider taking notes!). If you're writing a report, focus solely on that. No checking emails. No scrolling through social media. If you find this challenging, try doing calls with video on. When everyone can see you, it reduces the temptation to become distracted.

Plus, if you're having a one-on-one call with someone and aren't engaged, it is always going to be clear to the other person. They'll feel unimportant. If you're expecting an interruption during the interaction, tell the person at the beginning of the call. Otherwise, act as if you are sitting directly across from the person.

The Make-or-Break Virtual Skill

Now that we've covered the nuts and bolts of working remotely, let's talk about the no. 1 skill that will make or break your success as a remote worker: building relationships virtually. I covered this in depth in chapter 6, but as a refresher, the key tactics to develop relationships virtually are:

- Let your personality shine through—work shouldn't be all business, all the time.

- Be vulnerable. Admit when you don't know an answer or aren't sure how to proceed. Let your coworkers know if you've goofed up. Opening up like this will help your coworkers trust you.

- When you meet a coworker (in person or virtually) for the first time, don't dive straight into business. Get to know them on a personal level first.

- Learn how to handle difficult conversations so you maintain and build the relationship even through bumpy periods.

- Use video or phone calls to resolve contentious issues. Email won't be effective if the air needs to be cleared.

- Be a contributor. Share helpful content and respond to your coworkers' requests in a timely matter.

What to Do When Working Virtual Is an Option

As part of the Chicago team, I had become accustomed to working in a virtual office setting, where most interactions took place via phone. Then I relocated to the Seattle Business Unit, where there was a sizable team working in an office environment. It was quite an adjustment. As the office leader, I was expected to be mentally sharp and exude positive energy. All the time.

Some of the differences between virtual settings and office environments are obvious. In an office, communication occurs in passing ("over the watercooler"). Interactions are short and concise. There is also more social banter. Generally, there isn't an option to ignore people without appearing antisocial—very different from the virtual world, where I can let phone calls go to voicemail.

In the always-on office environment, I was exhausted by the end of the day. I wasn't ready for the activity level. Much like grandparents who love watching their grandkids, I got tired from having to be more attentive as well as the increased activity level around me. I now find it exhilarating working side-by-side with my Centric colleagues, but it certainly took some time getting used to.

—Ted G., Seattle, Washington

If you've gotten accustomed to working virtually, you may find it difficult to go back to an office environment. But if you have the option to work from your home *or* your company's office, you should do both.

You'll want to find the right mix of time to spend in each environment. Each has its advantages and tradeoffs. The following considerations will help you find your ideal formula:

- In my experience, given the option, most workers will choose to work from home most of the time. Research has found this to be true, as well.[6] If you're an individual contributor, however, you'll be a more effective team member if you have some presence in the company office, as face-to-face interactions are the most effective way to build deep relationships.

- During your office visits, focus on maintaining and building relationships. If you are a leader or supervisor, treat in-person meetings as a special opportunity to build team cohesion and relationships.

- When difficult conversations need to happen (like giving someone feedback), the conversation should be in person if possible.

Working with Customers When You Are Virtual

We were one of Centric's first customers. At the time, the idea of not having a "real" office was certainly uncommon. For us, it always begged the question, "In a virtual company, what's the dress code?"

As we began our initial engagements, whenever we'd interact over the phone with Centric team members, we'd often start discussions in a light-hearted fashion to break the ice. One question that often came up was "How did you dress today?" There were a lot of jokes about pajamas and lounge pants. Over time, as the relationship grew and we become more comfortable with the no-office model, we moved on from our preoccupation with their company dress code.

At the end of our first year working together, we were pleasantly surprised to receive a holiday package from Centric containing super soft Lands' End lounging pants embroidered with the Centric logo.

—Mark D., director of a multinational car manufacturer

When we first started 20 years ago, virtual work was new. We had to convince skeptical clients to work with us. Fast-forward to today: working with remote employees and teams is almost universally accepted.[7] Customers are space-constrained, and critical talent is hard to find; their own employees are demanding the ability to work remotely, and the tools we have today make remote work seamless.

We believe we'll all work virtually in the future. Until then, when you are working with a customer remotely, the following two tactics will make it easier.

First, if you anticipate interruptions (like a barking dog or a package delivery), acknowledge up front that you are working from home. Rarely is a client bothered by this anymore. If you have a super critical call where you don't want any interruptions, take the call from your car or make sure the house will be quiet. In some cases, I've nicely asked my wife to take everyone out, including the dog.

Second, video has become so common that around 80 percent of businesses use video for meetings.[8] If you're going to have a video call, you'll want to appear professional (at least from the waist up) and clean up the part of your workspace that's visible.

For clients who are not used to working with a virtual team, take the time to educate them on how to interact in a virtual setting. Most clients appreciate learning to work this way. We invite them to use our collaboration tools to allow us to interact more seamlessly.

Be a Culture Builder

Companies are only able to maintain great cultures because of the individuals who protect and promote the culture and help it evolve over time. You can greatly enhance your value by being a culture builder—even when you're part of a completely virtual organization.

Here's how.

Be a culture protector

When I lead the training class teaching our company's culture to new hires, I make sure everyone realizes they are now a protector of our culture. This means that once they understand what our culture is, each of them has the responsibility to keep our culture strong.

Know and live the core values

To have a great culture, companies must authentically live their core values. But they can't do that without each individual worker learning those values and applying them to their daily work. By doing this, your company's culture won't be the only thing being promoted—you probably will be as well!

Share ideas on how to improve the culture

Culture is never static, and ours is great because thousands of people have contributed ideas on how to make it better. Once you have a feel for the culture, share your thoughts on how to enhance it. Some of our best improvements have come from our newest employees who can see things from a fresh perspective.

Refer and hire culture fits

A culture falls apart once a company starts hiring new employees who aren't a culture fit. When you refer potential recruits or help with the hiring process, remember your role as culture protector. Ask yourself if you feel like the candidate has personality traits that naturally align with your culture. If you aren't sure about someone, speak up so your concerns can be investigated.

Quick Read Summary

- The biggest problem new virtual workers encounter is that they work too much.

- Most anyone can learn to be a great virtual employee. The top skills to learn are setting healthy boundaries between your work life and personal life and building relationships virtually.

- Think through the work environment and schedule that works for you. Many virtual employees use a mix of their home office, free spaces such as coffee shops, and a traditional office, whether it's their company's or a client's.

- You have the opportunity to help build and promote your company's culture by living the company's core values in your daily work and influencing who is hired.

How to Get Started Being a Great Virtual Worker

- Create healthy boundaries between your work and personal life.

- Find a space where you can work free of interruptions and distractions.

- You likely have some flexibility on when you can begin and end the workday, so structure your schedule around when you're the most productive.

- Stay connected with your coworkers by meeting up for coffee or quickly checking in online.

Challenges You Will Encounter

- If you don't set good boundaries, you may end up working far more than the typical 40-hour week.

- Your family or roommates might not initially understand that you need to be left alone while you're working at home. You need to communicate to them when you should not be disturbed, whether that's during certain hours or when you're sitting at your desk in your home office.

- It's tempting to multitask while you're on conference calls, but remaining present will make you and your team more effective.

- Although most clients are now used to working with remote teams, you may have to educate them on how to interact in a virtual
setting.

CONCLUSION

Building Culture Never Ends ˙

I found out I was pregnant with my first child just days after joining Centric. I was still trying to gain my footing at a new company, and now I was also nervous about becoming a mother. Little did I know, Centric is the best place to weather this life change. Although my coworkers are located all over the country, I felt the best "virtual hug" when I received a bundle in the mail full of goodies for our little one just days after returning home from the hospital. There was even a Centric onesie and Centric cap. I was amazed by the love I felt from folks miles and miles away.

—Heather B., St. Louis, Missouri

Culture building never stops. Once you have established a solid culture, you'll want to continue to nurture and grow it—otherwise its greatness won't last. Twenty years in, we have nearly 1,000 brilliant people who keep innovating and adding new ideas and traditions to our culture (like surprise gift baskets for all new babies joining the Centric family).

We treat our culture as seriously as we do our business strategy. Just like you would innovate on new business offerings, we do the same with our culture. We try out different ideas, see what is going to advance our culture, and then adopt what works.

As our original founders have started to retire, we have been using the concepts in this book, working to ensure our company culture is passed on to the next generation. We want to make sure our culture not only lives on but thrives in the future, for another 20 years and beyond.

You've Got This

I speak with a lot of executives who can't fathom how we operate a virtual company while also maintaining a great culture. Most think the two are mutually exclusive and believe it would never work in their own organization. Over the years, I've watched remote work slowly gain acceptance and have seen many companies build great cultures with remote teams—we're hardly alone in this new virtual era. And if the predictions are correct, the coronavirus pandemic will forever change how people work in many industries, ushering in an era of widespread acceptance of remote work.

Anyone can do this. It's not always easy work, but it's doable so long as it starts with company leaders who are passionate and make it a priority. Armed with the roadmap laid out in this book, you'll build a culture that not only wins awards but also makes your company somewhere you love working.

Personally, having a great company culture has brought meaning and happiness to my life. We are not a bunch of coworkers doing a job. We are a family that loves working together. Go build a culture you love.

ACKNOWLEDGMENTS

Our culture and all of the wisdom in this book is the culmination of so many people at Centric. I'm grateful to get to represent the company in writing this book, but I also want to clearly acknowledge that this is the work of many intelligent, committed people who have made Centric what it is today. This book is dedicated to the employees of Centric past and present who have all contributed to our unmatched culture. My heartfelt thanks for letting me represent you.

After coming up with the idea for this book, I wrote a first draft and asked for feedback from a few people at Centric. Most of the feedback could be summarized as "You are going to get a ghostwriter, right?" I was able to rally and write the book but want to offer a big thank you to the editors who actually understand the English language and made this immeasurably better. My thanks to Stephanie Zeilenga for the research and heavy editing, to Carolina VonKampen for the copyediting, book design, and publishing, and to Seanna Tucker for the overall management of the editing and publishing process.

APPENDIX

Centric Consulting Culture Awards 2008–2019

2019

Winner	*Comparably*: Best Company Culture
Winner	*Comparably*: Best Company for Women
Winner	*Columbus Business First* BizTech Awards: Outstanding Innovation
Winner	*Columbus Business First*: Ohio's Best Places to Work
Winner	*HR Tech Outlook*: Top 10 Change Management Consulting Services Companies
Listed	*Boston Business Journal*: Largest IT Consulting Firms in Massachusetts

Winner	*CIOReview*: Top 10 Most Promising BPM Consulting/Services Companies
Winner	NorthCoast 99: Best Places to Work in Northeast Ohio
Winner	*Louisville Business First*: Best Places to Work in Greater Louisville
Winner	*Crain's Chicago Business*: Chicago's 100 Best Places to Work in 2019
Winner	*Ohio Business Magazine*: 2019 Ohio Success Awards

2018

Winner	*Charlotte Business Journal*: Best Places to Work in Charlotte
Listed	*Boston Business Journal*: Largest IT Consulting Firms in Massachusetts
Winner	*Columbus Business First*: Best Places to Work in Columbus
Winner	NorthCoast 99: Best Places to Work in Northeast Ohio
Winner	*Louisville Business First*: Best Places to Work in Louisville
Winner	*Cincinnati Enquirer*: 2018 Top Workplace
Finalist	*Columbus Business First*: Corporate Citizenship
Winner	*Ohio Business Magazine*: Top 50 Best Places to Work in Ohio

Finalist   *St. Louis Business Journal*: Best Places to
                Work in St. Louis

2017

Winner   People Working Cooperatively (PWC):
                2017 Volunteer of the Year
Winner   *Columbus Business First*: Best Places to
                Work in Columbus
Winner   *Consulting Magazine*: 2017 Excellence
                in Social and Community Investment
                (with Apparo and Matthews HELP)
Winner   NorthCoast 99: Best Places to Work in
                Northeast Ohio
Honoree   *Inc.*: Inc. 5000 Hall of Fame
Winner   *Ohio Business Magazine*: Best Places to
                Work in Ohio
Finalist   University of Cincinnati Goering
                Center Family and Private Business
                Awards: Best Family and Private
                Business Practices
Listed   *The Muse*: Top 10 Amazing Companies
                That Are Hiring Right Now
Finalist   *Columbus Business First*: Corporate
                Caring Awards
Winner   *Louisville Business First*: Louisville's
                Best Places to Work
Winner   *Crain's Chicago Business*: Best Places to
                Work for Minorities

2016

Listed	Glassdoor: 9 Companies as Cool as Google—Hiring Now!
Listed	*Boston Business Journal*: Largest IT Consulting Firms in Massachusetts
Winner	NorthCoast 99: Best Places to Work in Northeast Ohio
Semifinalist	University of Cincinnati Goering Center Family and Private Business Awards: Best Family and Private Business Practices
Winner	Enquirer Media: 100 Top Workplaces in the Region (Cincinnati)
Winner	*Louisville Business First*: Louisville's Best Places to Work
Winner	Glassdoor: Highest Rated CEOs in 2016
Listed	*Forbes*: Best Management Consulting Firms in Digital Transformation and IT
Listed	*Forbes*: Best Management Consulting Firms in Technology
Listed	*Forbes*: Best Management Consulting Firms in Telecommunications
Winner	Glassdoor: Employee's Choice Award for Best Places to Work
Winner	*Inc.*: Inc. 5000 Fastest Growing Companies

2015

Winner	*Columbus Business First*: Best Places to Work in Columbus
Winner	NorthCoast 99: Best Places to Work in Northeast Ohio
Winner	Enquirer Media: Top 100 Workplaces in Cincinnati
Winner	*Inside Business Magazine*: 2015 NEO Success Award
Winner	*Inc.*: Inc. 5000 Fastest Growing Companies

2014

Winner	*Columbus Business First*: Best Places to Work in Columbus
Winner	NorthCoast 99: Best Places to Work in Northeast Ohio
Winner	*Inside Business Magazine*: 2014 NEO Success Award
Winner	*Smart Business Magazine*: Pillar Award for Community Service
Winner	*Inc.*: Inc. 5000 Fastest Growing Companies
Winner	*Inc.*: Top Job Creators in Ohio

2013

Winner	*Columbus Business First*: Best Places to Work in Columbus
Winner	NorthCoast 99: Best Places to Work in Northeast Ohio
Winner	*Inc.*: Inc. 5000 Fastest Growing Companies
Winner	*Inc.*: Top Job Creators in Ohio
Winner	*Inside Business Magazine*: 2013 NEO Success Award
Runner-up	BRIDGES for a Just Community and *Cincinnati Business Courier*: Tri-State Regional Workplace Inclusion Award

2012

Semifinalist	TechColumbus: Tech Columbus Innovation Awards
Winner	*Inc.*: Inc. 5000 Fastest Growing Companies
Winner	*Inside Business Magazine*: 2012 NEO Success Award
Patriot Award, Above and Beyond Award	Employer Support of the Guard and Reserve

2011

Winner   *Inc.*: Inc. 5000 Fastest Growing
                Companies

2010

Winner   *Inc.*: Inc. 5000 Fastest Growing
                Companies
Winner   *Consulting Magazine*: Top 10 Best
                Small Firms to Work For

2009

Winner   *Inc.*: Inc. 5000 Fastest Growing
                Companies

2008

Winner   *Inc.*: Inc. 5000 Fastest Growing
                Companies

NOTES

Introduction

1. Upwork, *Future Workforce 2019: How Younger Generations Are Reshaping the Future Workforce*, March 1, 2019, https://www.slideshare.net/upwork/future-workforce-2019-how-younger-generations-are-reshaping-the-future-workforce/1.
2. "Table 6. Employed persons working at home, workplace, and time spent working at each location by full- and part-time status and sex, jobholding status, and educational attainment, 2018 annual averages," U.S. Bureau of Labor Statistics, last modified June 19, 2019, https://www.bls.gov/news.release/atus.t06.htm.
3. Upwork, *Future Workforce 2019*.
4. OWLLabs, *State of Remote Work 2019*, September 2019, https://www.owllabs.com/state-of-remote-work/2019.
5. Randall Beck and Jim Harter, "Companies Are Missing Opportunities for Growth and Revenue," *Gallup News*, April 28, 2015, https://news.gallup.com/businessjournal/182912/companies-missing-opportunities-growth-revenue.aspx.

Chapter 1

1. CoSo Cloud, "CoSo Cloud Survey Shows Working Remotely Benefits Employers and Employees," February 17, 2015, https://www.cosocloud.com/press-releases/connectsolutions-survey-shows-working-remotely-benefits-employers-and-employees.

2. Jessica Rohman, *The Business Case for a High-Trust Culture* (San Francisco: Great Place to Work, 2016), https://s3.amazonaws.com/media.greatplacetowork.com/pdfs/Business+Case+for+a+High-Trust+Culture_081816.pdf.

3. Paul J. Zak, "The Neuroscience of Trust," *Harvard Business Review*, January–February 2017, https://hbr.org/2017/01/the-neuroscience-of-trust.

4. Nicholas Bloom et al., "Does Working from Home Work? Evidence from a Chinese Experiment," NBER Working Paper No. 18871, March 2013, https://www.nber.org/papers/w18871.pdf.

5. TINYpulse, *What Leaders Need to Know about Remote Workers*, 2016, https://www.tinypulse.com/what-leaders-need-to-know-about-remote-workers-report.

6. Kerry Patterson, Joseph Grenny, and Al Switzler, *Crucial Conversations* (New York: McGraw-Hill, 2012).

Chapter 2

1. Jim Collins and Jerry I. Porras, "Building Your Company's Vision," *Harvard Business Review*, Septem-

ber–October 1996, https://hbr.org/1996/09/build-ing-your-companys-vision.

2. David Burkus, "A Tale of Two Cultures: Why Culture Trumps Core Values in Building Ethical Organizations," *The Journal of Values Based Leadership* 4, no. 1 (Winter/Spring 2011), http://www.valuesbasedleadershipjournal.com/issues/vol4issue1/tale_2culture.php.

Chapter 3

1. Leigh Thompson, "Go ahead and tell your most embarrassing story. It will boost your creativity," *Fast Company*, September 20, 2019, https://www.fastcompany.com/90406432/go-ahead-and-tell-your-most-embarrassing-story-it-will-boost-your-creativity.

Chapter 4

1. Nick Otto, "Avoidable turnover costing employers big," *Employee Benefit News Magazine*, August 9, 2017, https://www.benefitnews.com/news/avoidable-turnover-costing-employers-big.

Chapter 5

1. Eleni Zoe, "Satisfaction with Onboarding: What New Hires Want," TalentLMS, August 22, 2019, https://www.talentlms.com/blog/new-employee-onboarding-study/.

2. Zoe, "Satisfaction with Onboarding."

3. LinkedIn, *2018 Workplace Learning Report*, 2018, https://learning.linkedin.com/resources/work-place-learning-report-2018.

4. Eagle's Flight, "Infographic: Experiential Learning and Organizational Development," *Organizational Training & Development Blog*, June 22, 2016, https://www.eagles-flight.com/blog/a-visual-guide-to-experiential-learning-for-organizational-development.

5. Heather Boushey and Sarah Jane Glynn, *There Are Significant Business Costs to Replacing Employees*, Center for American Progress, November 16, 2012, https://www.americanprogress.org/wp-content/uploads/2012/11/CostofTurnover.pdf.

6. Suzanne de Janasz and Maury Peiperl, "CEOs Need Mentors Too," *Harvard Business Review*, April 2015, https://hbr.org/2015/04/ceos-need-mentors-too.

7. "Return on Culture: Proving the connection between culture and profit," Grant Thornton, accessed April 1, 2020, https://www.grantthornton.com/returnonculture.

8. "Korn Ferry Leadership Architect™ Certification," Korn Ferry, accessed April 1, 2020, https://www.kornferry.com/solutions/products/hr-certification-korn-ferry-leadership-architect.

Chapter 6

1. Paul J. Zak, "The Neuroscience of Trust," *Harvard Business Review*, January–February 2017, https://hbr.org/2017/01/the-neuroscience-of-trust.

2. Zak, "The Neuroscience of Trust."

3. Francesca Gino, "Cracking the Code of Sustained Collaboration," *Harvard Business Review*, November–December 2019, https://hbr.org/2019/11/cracking-the-code-of-sustained-collaboration.

4. Lea Winerman, "E-mails and egos," *Monitor on Psychology* 37, no. 2 (February 2006), https://www.apa.org/monitor/feb06/egos.

Chapter 7

1. "Human Circuit—Conductors and Insulators," Steve Spangler Science, accessed April 1, 2020, https://www.stevespanglerscience.com/lab/experiments/human-circuit/.

2. Meetings Mean Business, *Small Business Survey Key Findings*, https://dev-meetingsmeanbusiness.pantheonsite.io/sites/default/files/MMB%20Small%20Business%20Survey%20Key%20Findings.pdf.

3. Ed Catmull, *Creativity, Inc.: Overcoming the Unseen Forces That Stand in the Way of True Inspiration* (New York: Random House, 2014).

4. Augusto Giacoman, "The Serious Fun of Shared Experiences at Work," *strategy + business*, November 7, 2016, https://www.strategy-business.com/blog/The-Serious-Fun-of-Shared-Experiences-at-Work?gko=05442.

5. General Stanley McChrystal, *Team of Teams: New Rules of Engagement for a Complex World* (New York: Portfolio, 2015).

6. Gareth Cook, "Why We Are Wired to Connect," *Scientific American*, October 22, 2013, https://www.scientifi-

camerican.com/article/why-we-are-wired-to-connect/.

7. Jim Harter, "Employee Engagement on the Rise in the U.S.," *Gallup News*, August 26, 2018, https://news.gallup.com/poll/241649/employee-engagement-rise.aspx.

8. Margee Kerr, Greg J. Siegle, and Jahala Orsini, "Voluntary arousing negative experiences (VANE): Why we like to be scared," *Emotion* 19, no. 4 (2019): 682–98, https://doi.org/10.1037/emo0000470.

9. Daniel Sgroi, *Happiness and Productivity: Understanding the Happy-Productive Worker*, Social Market Foundation, October 2015, https://www.ciphr.com/wp-content/uploads/2016/11/Social-Market-Foundation-Publication-Briefing-CAGE-4-Are-happy-workers-more-productive-281015.pdf.

10. Rachel Emma Silverman, "Workplace Distractions: Here's Why You Won't Finish This Article," *Wall Street Journal*, December 11, 2012, https://www.wsj.com/articles/SB10001424127887324339204578173252223022388.

11. Jim Harter and Amy Adkins, "Are Your Star Employees Slipping Away?" *Gallup Workplace*, February 24, 2017, https://www.gallup.com/workplace/236351/star-employees-slipping-away.aspx.

12. Karandeep Anand, "Deskless Not Voiceless: A new approach to connecting everyone within your business," Workplace by Facebook, accessed April 1, 2020, https://www.workplace.com/workplace/blog/deskless-not-voiceless.

13. Nina McQueen, "Workplace Culture Trends: The Key to Hiring (and Keeping) Top Talent in 2018," Linke-

dIn, June 26, 2018, https://blog.linkedin.com/2018/
june/26/workplace-culture-trends-the-key-to-hiring-
and-keeping-top-talent.

Chapter 8

1. Kevin Ruck, Mary Welch, and Barbara Menara, "Employee voice: An antecedent to organisational engagement?" *Public Relations Review* 43, no. 5 (December 2017): 904–14, https://www.sciencedirect.com/science/article/abs/pii/S0363811116304805.
2. "Developing and Sustaining Employee Engagement," SHRM, https://www.shrm.org/resourcesandtools/tools-and-samples/toolkits/pages/sustainingemployeeengagement.aspx.
3. Jim Asplund and Nikki Blacksmith, "The Secret of Higher Performance," *Gallup News*, May 3, 2011, https://news.gallup.com/businessjournal/147383/secret-higher-performance.aspx.
4. Nagesh Belludi, "To Inspire, Pay Attention to People: The Hawthorne Effect," *Right Attitudes*, May 27, 2016, https://www.rightattitudes.com/2016/05/27/to-inspire-pay-attention-to-people/.
5. Josh Bersin, "Feedback Is the Killer App: A New Market and Management Model Emerges," *Forbes*, August 26, 2015, https://www.forbes.com/sites/josh-bersin/2015/08/26/employee-feedback-is-the-killer-app-a-new-market-emerges/#5efa47d45edf.
6. Bersin, "Feedback Is the Killer App."
7. Sophia Bernazzani, "The Ultimate Guide to Your Net

Promoter Score (NPS)," HubSpot, September 13, 2019 (updated January 30, 2020), https://blog.hubspot.com/service/what-is-nps.

8. DecisionWise, *2018 State of Employee Engagement Report*, 2018, https://decision-wise.com/state-employee-engagement-report/.

9. Jackie Wiles, "Is It Time to Toss Out Your Old Employee Engagement Survey?" Gartner, November 26, 2018, https://www.gartner.com/smarterwithgartner/is-it-time-to-toss-out-your-old-employee-engagement-survey/.

10. Bersin, "Feedback Is the Killer App."

11. Gensler, *2013 U.S. Workplace Survey*, 2013, https://www.gensler.com/uploads/document/337/file/2013_US_Workplace_Survey_07_15_2013.pdf.

12. Amy Adkins and Brandon Rigoni, "Managers: Millennials Want Feedback, But Won't Ask for It," *Gallup Workplace*, June 2, 2016, https://www.gallup.com/workplace/236450/managers-millennials-feedback-won-ask.aspx.

13. Morley Winograd and Dr. Michael Hais, *How Millennials Could Upend Wall Street and Corporate America*, Governance Studies at Brookings, May 2014, https://www.brookings.edu/wp-content/uploads/2016/06/Brookings_Winogradfinal.pdf.

14. Karie Willyerd, "Millennials Want to Be Coached at Work," *Harvard Business Review*, February 27, 2015, https://hbr.org/2015/02/millennials-want-to-be-coached-at-work.

15. Deloitte, *Global Human Capital Trends 2016*, Deloitte University Press, 2016, https://www2.deloitte.com/

content/dam/Deloitte/global/Documents/Human-Capital/gx-dup-global-human-capital-trends-2016. pdf.

16. John Baldoni, "Employee Engagement Does More Than Boost Productivity," *Harvard Business Review*, July 4, 2013, https://hbr.org/2013/07/employee-engagement-does-more.

Chapter 9

1. Forrester, *The Total Economic Impact™ Of Microsoft Teams: Improved Employee And Company Performance*, April 2019, https://www.microsoft.com/en-us/microsoft-365/blog/wp-content/uploads/sites/2/2019/04/Total-Economic-Impact-Microsoft-Teams.pdf.

2. Gartner, "Gartner Says Worldwide Social Software and Collaboration Revenue to Nearly Double by 2023," September 24, 2019, https://www.gartner.com/en/newsroom/press-releases/09-24-2019-gartner-says-worldwide-social-software-and-collaboration-revenue-to-nearly-double-by-2023.

3. Janet Choi, "How Radical Transparency Kills Stress," *Fast Company*, July 15, 2013, https://www.fastcompany.com/3014160/how-radical-transparency-kills-stress.

4. Harvard Business Review Analytic Services, *The Impact of Employee Engagement on Performance*, *Harvard Business Review*, April 20, 2016, https://hbr.org/sponsored/2016/04/the-impact-of-employee-engagement-on-performance.

5. TINYpulse, "7 Vital Trends Disrupting Today's Work-

place: Results and Data from 2013 TINYpulse Employ-ee Engagement Survey," 2013, https://www.tinypulse.com/resources/employee-engagement-survey-2013.

6. Richard Bailey, "There Are Now 5 Generations in the Workforce—Can They Work Together?" *Fast Company*, February 7, 2019, https://www.fastcompany.com/90302569/there-are-now-5-generations-in-the-workforce-can-they-work-together.

7. Lori Wright and Natalie McCullough, "New survey ex-plores the changing landscape of teamwork," Microsoft 365, April 19, 2018, https://www.microsoft.com/en-us/microsoft-365/blog/2018/04/19/new-survey-explores-the-changing-landscape-of-teamwork/.

8. Jacob Morgan, "Why the Millions We Spend on Em-ployee Engagement Buy Us So Little," *Harvard Business Review*, March 10, 2017, https://hbr.org/2017/03/why-the-millions-we-spend-on-employee-engage-ment-buy-us-so-little.

Chapter 10

1. OWLLabs, *State of Remote Work 2019*, September 2019, https://www.owllabs.com/state-of-remote-work/2019.

2. University of Illinois at Urbana-Champaign, "Brief di-versions vastly improve focus, researchers find," *Science-Daily*, February 8, 2011, https://www.sciencedaily.com/releases/2011/02/110208131529.htm.

3. Ravi Mehta, Rui (Juliet) Zhu, and Amar Cheema, "Is Noise Always Bad? Exploring the Effects of Ambi-ent Noise on Creative Cognition," *Journal of Consumer*

Research 39, no. 4 (December 2012): 784–99, JSTOR, http://www.jstor.org/stable/10.1086/665048.

4. Paul Atchley, "You Can't Multitask, So Stop Trying," *Harvard Business Review*, December 21, 2010, https://hbr.org/2010/12/you-cant-multi-task-so-stop-tr.

5. Earl Miller, "Here's Why You Shouldn't Multitask, According to an MIT Neuroscientist," *Fortune*, December 7, 2016, http://fortune.com/2016/12/07/why-you-shouldnt-multitask/.

6. Buffer, *State of Remote Work*, 2019, https://buffer.com/state-of-remote-work-2019.

7. Buffer, *State of Remote Work*.

8. Lifesize, *2019 Impact of Video Conferencing Report*, 2019, https://www.lifesize.com/~/media/Documents/Related%20Resources/Guides/The%20Future%20of%20Video%20Communication%20and%20Meeting%20Productivity.ashx?la=en.

Larry English is president and cofounder of Centric Consulting, a management consulting firm that guides you in the search for answers to complex digital, business, and technology problems. Before Centric Consulting, Larry worked for a large international consulting firm out of college until he got burned out at 25. He and his newlywed wife backpacked around the world as he tried to find his path in life—and he did. Shortly after returning home, he and his like-minded pals founded Centric with a focus on changing how consulting was done by building a remote company with a mission to create a culture of employee and client happiness. Today, Centric is a 1,000-plus person company with offices in 12 US cities and India. Larry is father to four boys and husband to an adventurous wife. They reside in Columbus, Ohio.

Larry is donating a portion of the royalties he receives from *Office Optional* to charity. To learn more about him and how to become an office optional company, visit LarryEnglish.net.